Phoenix Warriors:

Rising From the Ashes of Domestic Violence

Stories of Courage, Survival, and the
Unbreakable Spirit of Those Who Refused to Be Silenced

By

Angels of Love

Phoenix Warriors: *Rising From the Ashes of Domestic Violence*
© 2025 Angels of Love

For permission requests, write to the publisher at:
Angels of Love
⊠ **Publishing Department**
1305 East Nolana Avenue, Suite D
McAllen, Texas 78504
Email: phoenixwarriorbook@gmail.com
Website: Angelsoflove.love
ISBN: 979-8-9998424-9-7

First Edition – 2025
Edited by Diane Carolyn Salinas
Phoenix Warrior Group photo by Cesar Toban
Printed in the United States of America

DISCLAIMER

This book contains real-life accounts and descriptions of domestic violence, abuse, and trauma that may be distressing or triggering to some readers. These stories are shared to raise awareness, honor survivors, and provide hope to those who may be experiencing or recovering from abuse. Reader discretion is strongly advised.

If you or someone you know is in immediate danger, call 911. For confidential help, call the National Domestic Violence Hotline at **1-800-799-SAFE (7233)** or text **"START"** to **88788**.

ACKNOWLEDGEMENTS

We at *Angels of Love* wish to express our deepest gratitude to the true heroes of this book — the courageous survivors who chose to share their deeply personal journeys in Phoenix Warriors: *Rising From the Ashes of Domestic Violence.* Your willingness to open your hearts and relive painful moments is an act of extraordinary bravery. Each of you has transformed your wounds into words with the hope that somewhere, a victim in silence will find the strength to speak, to seek help, and to believe that a new life is possible. Your stories are not only testaments of survival, but also beacons of hope, guiding others toward safety and healing.

We also extend our heartfelt thanks to Diane C. Salinas, member of the *Angels of Love* Advisory Council, whose generosity of heart, time, and talent brought these stories to life. Diane approached each narrative with compassion and care, ensuring that every survivor's voice was honored while shaping their words into a work that could reach the hearts of readers everywhere.

This book stands as a tribute to your strength, resilience, and the unbreakable spirit of those who refuse to be defined by their past. You are Phoenix Warriors, and the world is brighter because you chose to *rise*.

It is an honor to be a part of "Phoenix Warriors: *Rising from the Ashes of Domestic Violence*" as your Editor.

Thank you, Della, for inviting and trusting me to join you and *Angels of Love* in this momentous endeavor–especially for its inaugural anthology.

From meek-to-mavens, from career professionals to entrepreneurs and businesswomen…to "Thrivers", I am blown away not only by the stories told, as many are made-for-tv/movie worthy, but by each and every person who had the courage to share and transform their personal traumas into triumphs!

Thank you all for showing up and showing how…one courageous step at a time. Our hope is that by sharing your stories, others will be educated, inspired, and empowered to rise for FREEDOM from Abuse.

Most sincerely,

Diane C. Salinas

"Be FIERCELY Kind and Kindly FIERCE!"

©

A NOTE TO OUR READERS

The stories within these pages are raw, real, and courageous. They speak of heartbreak, fear, and the unthinkable—yet also of resilience, strength, and the power to rise again. In sharing their journeys, our Phoenix Warriors have chosen to shine a light on the darkness of domestic violence so others might find their own path to freedom and healing.

Please be advised: some passages contain sensitive content and descriptions of violence that may be upsetting or triggering. We encourage you to care for your heart and mind as you read. Take breaks when needed. Reach out for support if emotions rise to the surface.

If you or someone you know is living with abuse, you are not alone. Help is available.

Contact the National Domestic Violence Hotline at
1-800-799-SAFE (7233) or **text "START" to 88788**.

You are Strong, You are Worthy. And like the Phoenix, You are a Warrior, and you too, can Rise from the Ashes.

10 INTENTIONS FOR THIS BOOK

1. To give voice to the lived experiences of survivors who have endured and overcome the trauma of domestic violence.

2. To honor and memorialize those who did not survive, ensuring their stories and spirits are never forgotten.

3. To offer hope, strength, and encouragement to victims who are still in unsafe or harmful situations.

4. To raise awareness and break the silence surrounding domestic violence within communities.

5. To educate the public about the realities, warning signs, and long-term impacts of abuse.

6. To inspire action and advocacy in the fight to end domestic violence.

7. To provide a platform for survivors to reclaim their narratives and find healing through storytelling.

8. To show the resilience, courage, and transformation possible after leaving an abusive relationship.

9. To connect victims, survivors, and allies to resources and support networks.

10. To further the mission of *Angels of Love* in creating a future where safety, dignity, and respect are the norm for all.

DEDICATION

This book is dedicated to all the Phoenix Warriors who did not live to tell their story or to complete their story—those whose voices were silenced too soon, yet whose courage and spirit continue to inspire.

It is also dedicated to Maria Guadalupe "Lupita" Herrera, a faithful *Angels of Love* Board Member and Warrior who embodied the heart and mission of the organization. Lupita's unwavering commitment, compassion, and selflessness touched countless lives. Though she did not live to see this book come to fruition, her light and legacy shine brightly in every page.

May these stories honor your strength, preserve your memory, and ignite hope for those still fighting to rise from the ashes and be a beacon of hope for all who are still finding their wings.

FOREWORD

At *Angels of Love*, we have witnessed both the deepest wounds that domestic violence can inflict and the extraordinary strength it takes to rise above them. Each day, we meet survivors whose journeys are marked by unimaginable pain but also by breathtaking resilience. It is for them—and for every voice that has ever been silenced—that this book Phoenix Warriors: Rising From the Ashes of Domestic Violence was born.

This book is more than a collection of stories; it is a testament to survival, courage, and the unbreakable spirit that lives within each survivor. Like the mythical phoenix, these amazing female warriors have risen from the ashes of trauma, reclaiming their lives with dignity and determination. Their experiences shed light on the realities of abuse, but they also illuminate the power of healing, the hope of renewal, and the unwavering truth that no one is alone in this fight.

We recognize that these pages contain sensitive and, at times, painful accounts. They may stir emotions, reopen memories, or challenge perceptions. Yet, they also hold space for inspiration, understanding, and a call to action—for communities, families, and advocates to stand together against the epidemic of domestic violence.

To the brave individuals who have shared their stories here: your voices will echo far beyond these pages, breaking barriers of silence and igniting hope in those still struggling to find their way out. You are the living proof that healing is possible and that every survivor has the right to not just survive, but to thrive.

From all of us at *Angels of Love*, we dedicate this work to every Phoenix Warrior—past, present, and future. May it serve as a beacon for those still searching for the light and as a reminder to the world that from even the deepest ashes, new life can and will rise.

—Angels of Love

The Phoenix Warriors

Photo credit: Cesar Toban
Location: The Chateau on 5th, McAllen, Texas

Table of Contents

DANIELA'S Story...

Our family home was always filled with laughter, friends, and love. Growing up, our house was the go-to-hangout spot. It was a place where friends and family felt welcome and safe. I am one of seven children. My siblings and I had a joyful, close-knit childhood, guided by parents who did their best to protect us from the unpleasantness of the outside world.

My parents showed and modeled a Christian home with values and love. We spent a lot of time at church and at youth fellowship events. My mom was involved in youth and children's ministry, while Dad was actively involved in the community and church. We are a very blessed family in every sense of the word.

I met my ex-husband in the summer of my senior year. We were friends first and later became high school sweethearts. He had a car, a job, and more freedom than my parents allowed me. My home life was quite different from his. I didn't know much about his family at first. His parents were much older than mine; plus, he and his sibling were adopted. Sadly, he abruptly learned about his adoption from a friend in junior high.

I've always felt his issues might have stemmed from feeling abandoned and lied to, which I understand many adoptees experience and consider themselves so different from others.

When I was seventeen, I got pregnant in my senior year. My life changed drastically as I graduated early and got married at nineteen. My parents stepped in and took care of my oldest while I started college. A few years later, two more children were born.

In 2005, I became a licensed insurance agent and worked in our family business, which later provided the finances to allow my ex to start his company.

By 2013, I had opened my own insurance agency. I was juggling a lot: three kids, a new business, a home, and a marriage that was starting to unravel. My husband never hit me, but the emotional abuse, gaslighting, and financial manipulation were relentless. He was never faithful and never truthful. I was drowning.

He never kept his word, nor his promises, what he *did* do was drive around with one of his many secret lovers to San Antonio, Texas while I was working and taking care of our kids. I hired an investigator to follow him, who confirmed that he indeed had a female passenger with him. I knew it! I sensed something was off, but I needed to see it for myself. So, I drove to where the investigator told me I could find him. He tried blocking me from seeing his female passenger, until we had to stop at a traffic light.

With tears streaming down my face, I looked him straight in the eyes. He knew, I knew. To my surprise, with no remorse, he shot the finger at me! I was never so angry. It was ON! His *reckoning was* coming.

I cut in front of his Range Rover and drove straight home crying. In my rage, I tossed out all his belongings and vowed to be rid of him for good.

My kids, seeing how angry I was, were shocked and wanted to know what was going on. In my pain and frustration, I told them what I saw and his reaction to seeing me. This upset the kids, which turned the whole house into chaos.

As I was collecting his belongings, the kids removed family photos all over the house, from the hallway, and living room. It was at that moment that we all realized that we didn't have a *picture-perfect* family we thought we had. It broke my heart into a million pieces. It brought me to my knees; he had completely diminished and destroyed everything we worked so hard to achieve together.

He picked up his clothing and such, from the backyard and moved out for about six months. Right or wrong, in the name of keeping the family together, I eventually let him come back home. I really tried to make it work, but he was up to no good; he "hooked up" with our sixth grader's friend's mom, taking her on an out-of-town trip!

I immediately informed my parents and sister, my best friend, assistant, and attorney that there would be divorce proceedings. My parents were stunned, and brokenhearted hearing about his cheating. I had not told my family any details of his past mistakes. They, too, thought we had the picture-perfect marriage.

Shortly after that meeting with the attorney, I went ahead and filed for divorce. It took two long years to finalize. In the meantime, old habits die hard. Ever the romantic, I started seeing him off and on. He even made "good night" calls with the kids when he traveled to San Antonio for business.

One evening, he was travelling again and unbeknownst to him, he was on speaker. With my kids present, he started rudely answering my questions and swearing at me for calling him while he was out. I knew he was out-and-about as I could hear the sports bar ambiance in the background.

Hurt and embarrassed, I let him know that the kids could hear him. He quickly changed his voice. The kids spoke to him as usual, but the look on their faces changed when they heard the tone he used as he continued talking to me. The marriage was pretty much over for us then.

With all the womanizing and verbal abuse, my kids told me it was okay with them if I wanted to go through with the divorce. All the kids left the room, except for one child. The child he hurt the most. The one who "needed her Daddy's love." She said in her soft voice, "Mommy, please don't divorce Daddy! I don't want to be like the other kids at school." I couldn't bear to see her go through any more rejection, so I stayed. Once again, I tried everything to make the marriage work.

So, we eventually went to marital therapy. His complaint was that I was tough on him and the kids, and how I took over the *manly* reigns in the house. My defense was that I had to be the disciplinarian, while he played the *Disney Dad.* So, I went ahead and gave up those responsibilities and let him pay the bills. As usual, he disappointed us: the lights, water, and cable services got shut off! He was so unreliable, and it affected the whole family.

Up to this point I hadn't asked God for help. I approached a priest at my church, and I told him what was going on. His stance? *"Boys will be boys. Stop trying to be his mother."* I was dumbfounded! I couldn't believe those words would come out of a man of God. It was then that I totally lost faith in the Catholic Church. I mean, who says *that*?

Meanwhile, my ex had run his business to the ground owing money. Many times, I was stuck paying his debts. We were married, so I felt obligated to pay these people back. At one point, I had three big well-dressed *thugs* come to my office and demanded that I pay $6,500.00! When I asked why, all they said was that my ex wrote a hot check and they were there to collect.

What do you do at that moment except write the check?! This was one of many tough and scary situations he placed me in. It was exhausting! I remember saying to myself, "I just want to *breathe*."

The proverbial last straw was when I wanted to join him on one of his planned business trips to Las Vegas, Nevada. He emphatically nixed the idea. Something felt off about how he was acting. I remember asking God if there is something that I needed to see, to show me. The very next morning, at my ex's request, I took three signed checks to take care of a transaction for his business affairs at his bank. A friend of mine, who happened to work there, assisted me. After viewing his account, she asked how I had liked the Eilan Hotel stay in San Antonio. I told her I hadn't been there recently. She got quiet, which made me wonder what was showing up on the screen.

After leaving the bank, I immediately called the hotel for a copy of the billing statement. The lady asked if I wanted it to be emailed to the email address on file. I asked which email address it was, and it turned out to be one I had never heard of. I quickly wrote it down and asked her to email it to my personal email instead. After two attempts, I cracked his email password, and I couldn't believe what I saw. Multiple reservations and flights out of San Antonio for not one, but *two* women passengers, including their *names* with luxury retail shopping and fancy restaurant charges. I saw what I needed to know, and the reason my banking friend had been awkwardly quiet. It all made sense now. With printouts in hand, I instructed my attorney to set a divorce court date.

I went back to the bank and withdrew most of the money in his business account leaving $800 in it for him to fly home. I had made sure someone held the withdrawn money for safekeeping, and that he'd get it back when he returned. I didn't want him spending his client's money on those two women. I had his clothes packed in his truck and had it driven to the family ranch. I changed the locks, security alarm and codes at the house, and made sure to register his guns with the police. I then dropped off his guns at my attorney's office for safekeeping.

I was *done*. I had enough. I didn't shed another tear over him. I was so disappointed and beyond furious.

He called me early that afternoon. I never let on that I knew about the women and card charges, acting as if nothing happened. I also made sure I didn't take his next call until I had withdrawn his money and knew the bank would soon close.

At 6pm, he calls in a cheerful voice. The kids were in the car with me unaware of what I found out earlier in the day. I clearly remember him saying that he had a "great day" and asked me how my day went. Let's just say, I wasn't polite nor sweet as I told him to have fun with the two *wh@res* he was flying with that night! In his usual self, he lied and told me I was crazy.

I then let him know that I had found out about *everything,* and that I withdrew all his money out of his account. He sneered, demanding that I'd better deposit the money back immediately. Instead, I gave him less than 24 hours to fly back home, or that we were finished. My little ones were shocked and so sad. They sat quietly in the back seat as I drove home.

A barrage of calls came in 10-minutes apart threatening to kill me. Taking the threats seriously, I reported it to the police and my attorney. *Three* days later, police were waiting for him at the airport, but he somehow eluded them. They eventually pulled him over on his way to pick up our kids, who were at my sister's house. My eldest daughter was upset that I had called the police on her dad, but I told her we were all concerned by his threats and couldn't take a chance.

His excessive swearing at me continued. I never thought he would turn into someone so hateful. I think of myself as a strong person. But when it came to him, I was weak. I thank God for giving me strength to be steadfast in my integrity, as my ex-husband asked me many times to financially compromise my business and clients. I never gave in. I was committed to protecting every one of my clients and myself from him and his nefarious dealings. I was honest and realized what he was doing wasn't right. His cheating, manipulating, and lying is what caused our divorce. It was overwhelming for everyone involved.

Unfortunately, the story got even worse *after* our July 2015 divorce! Verifiable from police reports, my ex had slashed my car tires, turned off A/C breakers outside, broke into my house, and planted cameras and microphones on my bedroom wall and A/C vents! I remember being suspicious of him when he repeated comments that *I* had previously spoken to other people. It turned out he also had put GPS trackers on my cars as he kept appearing at events I was attending. How could you feel *safe* in your own home? What happened next almost took me over the edge.

After visiting a client, I was on my way to my office, I caught a highway ramp and noticed a car driving up right next to me. As I turned to look at it, I saw that the passenger had a gun pointed *right at me*, hammer pulled! I immediately floored it. They chased me at speeds of over ninety miles an hour! There were no police in sight. Suddenly, my phone rang, and my ex-husband's name appeared on the screen. I answered his call.

I shouted that I was being chased and asked him to *please* call 911 on 3-way. He just kept telling me that *it was going to be okay*. After about five frantic minutes of dodging other drivers and trying to escape the gunman's view, I quickly exited. The gunman's car stayed on the highway as I got away. I pulled into the nearest parking lot and had a full-blown panic attack. My ex continued calling, non-stop. Ignoring his calls, I delivered the papers to my office. Concerned, my dad asked me if I was okay? I divulged nothing. I got home and cried hysterically, telling no one that I just had a gun pointed at me in a high-speed car chase. Never in my life have I been that scared. It was like a scene straight out of an episode of *"Criminal Minds"* tv show; except *I lived it!* Turns out my ex-husband had been arrested for theft and other charges during and after our divorce. He brought it upon himself. Unfortunately, not without collateral damage.

One early morning, with police backup, an investigator pushed in my front door without a warrant, they rushed in to search my house for my ex and accused me of harboring him. I told them that he didn't live here anymore. The investigator relentlessly searched the whole house, every room, bathroom, attic, and closet. I wasn't hiding him, or lying, so I let them search the house. My daughter's friend, taking a shower at the time, was told to step out of the bathroom in case he was hiding in there. With everything going on I was praying they would find him so that my life would finally be easier without him. Luckily, he was eventually found and arrested soon after.

In December of 2017, my ex-husband's girlfriend unexpectedly came to my house with a puppy that he got for my daughter. I told the girlfriend that my oldest daughter had stopped by their apartment and saw an eviction notice on their door; I showed her a picture of it. His girlfriend had no idea; she became another victim of his lies. Panicked, she asked us to help her move out of their apartment!

While there, I came across FIVE loan applications for $20,000 *each* with a social security number that belonged to our 15-year-old son. You can imagine our reaction. What kind of father does that to his son? He heartlessly ruined my son's credit with a car purchase and multiple charges. The credit bureau requirement to clear my son's credit record was to file charges; I did so, immediately.

Matters turned from bad to worse to *strange* as my kids searched their dad's apartment garage and found pictures of me with my eyes burned out, candles, and prayers on paper. It looked like a shrine except it was one for witchcraft. The kids were stunned by all the things they had found. It was the first time they'd seen anything like it.

I wish I could say everything turned out for the better, but on Christmas 2019, the flu hit our family hard. We cancelled our Christmas family gathering as our extended family members were sick. I dragged my kids outside to clean up the yard. My best friend came over to help as she always did. My son, who was raking leaves, found a mysterious mason jar with a picture of me filled with black oil, and other disturbing things buried in our backyard. She picked it up and said, "Daniela, this is not good; it's a form of witchcraft. Now, you *need* to pray." They also found a Santa Muerte card in a white plastic bag under a bush as my kids tore up the yard.

All I could say to myself was, on *"Again?!"* My aunt, a mighty prayer warrior, arrived, and let me tell you, at that point I needed all the prayers I could get.

As if that wasn't enough, in January 2020, I was block-walking as I was campaigning for a local office. I approached a home and a man said he knew me. He went on to tell me, "I used to follow you." I just stood there in total shock. He told the story of my ex hiring him to trail me. I asked him if I could come back later to continue our conversation. I arrived with a meal for him as he went into details of my whereabouts. He asked me if I knew that my ex believed he was the beneficiary of my life insurance. He also revealed that he knew the man who my ex-husband had hired to *kill me*, not once, but *twice*.

I escaped the first attempt, hence the 2015 car-chase; the second time, the order was called off as my children were with me. The instructions were to shoot only if I was alone. Beyond stunned to hear what he was saying, I asked the man if he could come to my house and tell my children what he told me. Soon after, I sat my kids down, and he told them everything. I felt they were old enough to know the truth. I wanted them to hear exactly what happened and what their father was capable of. They were shell-shocked and so enraged at the same time. It was crazy at how everything was being revealed to us and confirmed what I already knew. My ex-husband was a homicidal sociopath. The realization that I was married to that kind of man was chilling.

Before the divorce, my ex was incredibly involved with the kids, giving of his time, coaching sports, and buying gifts. After the divorce, he was secretive and dishonest, to them and me. It also caused me to suffer financially. To avoid any potential fallout for my family, I was forced to pay off his debt, which left me feeling more alone and anxious. I never felt safe. I never felt like I could breathe. It was always one thing or another. There were several instances when a car would suspiciously park outside of our house. What we didn't know was that we, the kids and I, were also being followed. It was nerve-wracking to think it happened at all.

Our triggers? His was my calling him out on his lies; I found myself triggered by being lied to. Though I was not abused physically, the pain I felt was like the first time I found out about his infidelities. Add to that, *everything* else, it took the light out of my eyes. My heart wasn't just broken; it was shattered into pieces. To this day, he doesn't know that I know about his secret dealings and plots to end my life. God is so great. He has never left me and has always protected me.

It is safe to say, *trust* is a bit of an issue for me, and my walls go up every time I meet someone new. I refuse to depend on anyone else. I *do* look forward to meeting the right person. I've asked God to put him in my life in His timing. It took self-reflection, counseling, and God saving and helping me through it all.

As I reflect over those years, I was once quite naïve and wanted my family to be together at all costs; *no* matter what the price. But I'm wiser now. I had to be tough and disciplined at times because I had no other choice. Divorcing him almost cost me my life.

Many people have asked how I got through it all. The answer to that question is God. I started attending Tuesday night church service and completely surrendered myself to God. Being in the presence of the Lord, and feeling my heavenly Father's love, has enabled me to forgive my ex and move on with my life. It is because of God's grace and favor that has indeed kept me alive and thriving.

I've recently sold my business and closed that huge chapter in my life. I asked the Lord for his guidance and to lead me to my next steps. I now proudly serve as the Director of Development at *Angels of Love,* and a newly commissioned Chaplain. I have found my passion for giving back to women who have walked through "fire" in ways that no one else can imagine, if only to show that with God everything is possible.

---My VICTORY Statement---

For a long time, my story lived in silence.

Not because it didn't matter, but because

I was too ashamed to speak it.

Too afraid to be judged, too afraid no one would believe me.

But today, I broke the silence.

I lived through nights filled with fear and days filled with pretending.

I smiled when I was hurting.

I stayed when I wanted to run.

But here I am. Still standing, still breathing

and finally FREE.

It has made me who I am…

A woman of God

A warrior of strength and truth

A survivor who found her voice.

---Daniela---

LeANNA'S Story...

On the outside, I was someone who had it all together. I grew up in a devout Christian home with a mom and dad who had a loving marriage and were great parents.

I had a love of learning and graduated in the top 10% of my high school class in 2003. I then went on to graduate with a bachelor's; and earned my master's degree in social work by 2011. Yes, I was a very accomplished young lady in my twenties but was quite lonely. I wanted someone to share my life with and got a bit impatient meeting a man online.

I fell in love, or so I thought. As quickly as I fell for him, I found myself pregnant and married soon after. Unfortunately, it wasn't long before I realized he was not "The One". He struggled with heavy addictions. His anger and brokenness caused him to rage against me. Though I became very scared I stood up to him and never backed down, but it made the marriage even more toxic. Things went from bad to worse.

May 2012, I lost Nathan James, my first-born son, in my fifth month of pregnancy, through stillbirth. Seven months later, married for half a year, my husband was sent to prison for crimes committed prior to our marriage! One would think without him that my life would be better, but those 23 months were *Hell*.

Through the years, I worked as a case worker at a juvenile detention center; I was a special education teacher, a school social worker and a hospice/medical social worker. Hence, in my 40 years of life, I had seen many journeys and heard about trauma, the worst of the worst. Yet, it took me ten years AFTER my marriage to finally see that I, myself had LIVED through my own trauma of abuse and violence. His imprisonment was just the tip of the iceberg.

His incarceration fueled the emotional and verbal abuse towards me. Financial abuse was reversed as I, being the breadwinner, had to spend thousands of dollars on his commissary budget, phone calls and the cost of prison trips. All the while, he continued to angrily manipulate and control me, even in prison.

It didn't make sense on many levels. He should have been grateful, and I should have been stronger, as I had the upper hand. It didn't help that I was receiving death threats through it all. I believe the fear and pure stress of his being away was far worse than having him at home as you'll see why.

He was released from prison in September 2014, but I was *not* relieved, I knew the horror would continue, and it did. The violence picked up, he would throw things and break anything and everything: televisions, lamps, dishes, or computer screens; we ended up having numerous holes in our walls.

It was lonely to never have my immediate family over as I was too embarrassed for them to find out about what I was going through. I was stuck with him thinking I was being a "godly married woman". I found myself in deep depression and wrecked with high anxiety. I soon became a workaholic, being overwhelmed with my caseload of hospice patients. I traveled up to 140 miles one way, in one day. It was exhausting and saddening.

I cried, missed work, overslept, and isolated myself; it was then that I started to have suicidal ideations as I hated my life. I resorted to self-harming by cutting and emotional eating. Three months after his release in December 2014, I voluntarily admitted myself into a behavioral center for a week. The depression and anxiety had officially taken over my life; I was afraid of my own self; afraid that I was capable of truly hurting myself in my desperation.

Along with the abuse, rejection and neglect, I felt isolated and hid my horrible abusive marriage from my family and friends. Regret, shame and loneliness were the root of my depression. It got so bad that I was afraid to be left alone. I was afraid that I might harm myself and end it all. I went home right before Christmas. Medicated, I functioned to the best of my ability.

After acquiring some education and training, my husband decided he wanted a "new start" in his hometown of Houston, Texas. I searched for a job and secured a place for us to live. I pretended to be excited but, it would be a six-hour drive one-way away from my family, I was devastated and scared.

March 2015 was the month that we settled in Houston, and my new job began. July also marked the time when I found out about his infidelity via his text messages. It was July 4th, he, in drunken anger got physical as he wrapped his hands around my neck and choked me for the very first time. I narrowly blacked out but fought back, kicking and punching. I didn't back down. I then despised him and hated my marriage; I became *homicidal*.

I was distraught, broken, and betrayed. Thank God for Jennifer, my best friend from back home. She single-handedly kept me out of jail. I called her crying; she talked me down from making the gravest mistake and spoke life and hope into me. I hung on to her words and my faith in God.

It was short-lived when we tried to keep the marriage together, as he began drinking heavily again, and I'll never forget the night. We went to a bar, and he got so drunk that he started to hallucinate that I was leaving with two imaginary men. I tried to escape his on-coming rage. I ran or

I attempted to run outside to our car as he grabbed me by my hair and punched me in the back of my head.

I was shocked that he now was willing to abuse and attack me in public. It was then I realized I wasn't ever going to be safe with him again. That fear and realization immediately put me into a trance of terror, as my marriage continued.

I had to "walk on eggshells" to not trigger him. He was strong and of big stature, and I knew what he could do to me physically. My mental health struggled and gravely worsened when I lost my job in November 2016. I dragged myself back to the Valley with this person I now feared, in tow. The years blurred together, I lived in abuse *mode*.

Though I was close to my family, they had zero idea about my deep struggles, physically and emotionally. They only knew I was *unhappy*. Days and months turned into years, and I became pregnant in December 2018. I was so scared. I knew I was bringing a baby into a toxic abusive home, and that it was going to be difficult.

I had a very high-risk pregnancy and went to multiple doctor appointments completely alone as my husband was not involved. He worked out-of-town; he partied and drank all throughout my pregnancy. I gave birth, and the challenges escalated as I felt deserted finding proof of more infidelity, shortly thereafter. I endured deep post-partum depression and severe anxiety.

After the birth of our second son in July 2019, the deep hurt and pain resurfaced yet again, finding proof of an escort service purchased by my abuser, my then husband. I found out that he wasn't the only one I had to worry about. We were receiving death threats by supposed cartel members as he was being extorted for money from the escort.

My life, my family and my newborn son were now in danger. I once again fell into deep depression at the beginning of 2020. With the pandemic at an all-time panic throughout the world, the walls of my own world and home were falling in on me.

I prayed often, and at times it felt like it was a sin against God for me to pray for my own freedom; to pray for my spouse to release me from this covenant, and to free me from this life. It was so miserable, and the trauma deepened daily. I prayed to God to please let him peacefully go.

Every time I asked to leave him, or for us to separate and divorce, he threatened to hurt himself, me, and my *dog*! In my professional experience as a social worker, I was so afraid he would successfully harm himself and that I would be liable for his mental health crisis and demise. I began to pray for a fast way out…a safe way out.

One day in 2021, driving on the expressway in Harlingen, Texas, he turned to me and asked me if I was happy. I was so afraid that, depending on my answer, he would accelerate and kill us both, so, my voice shook as I told him, "No", that I was not happy. I told him I no longer felt safe. "Please," I told him, "…let's separate, let's get a divorce and go our separate ways." To my astonishment, he agreed. God had answered my prayers. He gave me a safe way out.

Fast forward, January 2021 was the last straw. I came to find out, yet again, of his high-risk sexual misbehavior, another affair. I left important documents, a couple of hundred dollars, and some clothes at my best friend's house and told her my plan to get an apartment and start over. March 16th, 2021, I filed for divorce and moved out in April.

As most statistics show, once a person decides to leave a domestic violent situation the chances of their abusers hurting them go up, as it was in my situation. Even though I left him, I still had to share a child with this toxic and violent person. He threatened to burn, torture, and drag me by a truck and beat me with a bat; my mind was in such fear and torment. I knew what this person was capable of.

Every single meet-up was public. Every single time I had a family member on the phone with me. Someone had my location everywhere I went; all the while covering my son in prayer as my abuser had his assigned custodial weekends.

I documented *everything*. I had made a police report about what was happening to me, the harassment, and terroristic threats. I went to the District Attorney's (DA's) office, and was told, "I'm sorry, ma'am, there's no recent proof of physical or sexual abuse." I was turned away with a stack of resources and pamphlets, *Angels of Love* was one of them. I felt defeated, so I surrounded myself with my tribe. I prayed fervently and educated myself. I was at a breaking point and God made a promise to me that *I would not die*. I was scared, but He promised that not only would I not die but that I would *survive* and *thrive*.

Now, it's 2025, I am blessed beyond measure. I have a stable, healthy relationship with my son. I am happily remarried to the man of my dreams. "Tristan, I love doing Life with you!" I continue to be a successful medical case management social worker. I serve at church and volunteer with numerous community agencies. I give back to thrive and serve my purpose. I specifically now serve on the *Angels of Love* Advisory Board. (It all started with a pamphlet from the District Attorney's office!)

For some reason God has kept me alive. I am thankful for the *Angels of Love* organization for bringing light to survivors of domestic violence and offering numerous programs to the community to break the cycle of abuse, and to prevent unhealthy relationships all together through education and services.

--My VICTORY Statement...

I felt defeated, so I surrounded myself with my tribe. I prayed fervently and I educated myself. I was at a breaking point and God made a promise to me that I would not die. I was scared, but He promised that not only would I not die but that I would
survive and *thrive*.

---LeAnna---

CHELSEA'S Story...

My dad left us when I was five years old. He had been in and out of my life…mostly, out. Mom was the sole provider. She was both parents to me and my baby sister who passed away at 18 months old when I was five. I never knew what a healthy relationship was supposed to be. To discipline, my mom would tell me *"Te pego porque te quiero."* ("I hit you because I love you.")

I met my boyfriend, Matt through mutual friends; I was just 15 or 16 years old. He was a 19-year-old and had already graduated from high school. Things were fine at first, but a few months of dating his behavior started to change. He became more possessive and texted me excessively. He would ask where I was and call me a liar when I told him I was with my family. I'd have to have my cousins or anyone else with me at the time to talk to him and convince him otherwise. I wish I had listened when people told me that his vibe was *off*…but I was "in love" and ignored their warnings.

What started as playful wrestling turned to where hits were getting harder, more painful. He must have heard the same saying as my mom did, which is why I didn't see the warning signs and accepted it as natural interaction. After six months he started showing jealous behavior accusing me of "checking out" everyone. He became angry and suspicious.

A year later is when he first hit me; he punched me. We got into an argument, I don't even remember what it was about, but he picked up a heavy book and threw it at me, hitting me in the right temple, leaving a huge bump on my forehead. I stayed at his house for two straight days so that my mom wouldn't know he was being abusive.

This might age me but, I was on Myspace and saw messages that he was writing to other women. I confronted him about it. He denied it and tried to make me think *I was crazy*. Turns out he was a serial cheater and projected all the blame on me. *If I were a better girlfriend he wouldn't mistreat or hit me*, he'd say…that *I deserved it*. In his mind he was the victim.

We dated off and on for two years. He would constantly ask me where I was as he drove by my house to check to see if my mom's car was in the driveway. I once looked out of my window and caught him driving by. I messaged him, and he admitted that he was passing by just to check to see if I was home as I had said. I asked him why, and his answer was that he *loved me*. He really tested those words.

One night, I didn't want to leave the party we were at. He grabbed me by my shoulder, squeezing my arm so hard that it left a mark. *"We're leaving,"* he said as he dragged me to his car all the while smacking me. I asked him why he thought it was okay to hit me, instead of answering he went on to accuse me of cheating with his friend and told me that I was nothing but a "whore." Frantically trying to talk him down, I told him he was the only one I loved. He continued hitting me on the drive home, side-punching me, one punch after another.

On another night out, John, a guy who had liked me in the past recognized me and noticed that I wasn't having fun as Matt had left me at our table alone for quite a long time. Matt, a few feet away, noticed that John was staring at me. John came up to me as my ex-boyfriend was walking towards me. Matt seemed a bit off, and suspicious that there was something going on between John and me.

My friend Isabella witnessed the whole scene as both men were coming towards me from different corners of the room. Matt grabbed my arm, seething at me that we were leaving, and again, calling me a "whore". John stepped in and they got into a fistfight. Angrier than I had ever seen him, my ex grabbed me to leave as my friends were trying to hold on to me, threatening to him that they'd call my mom.

That night, my friends asked what exactly was going on. I told them what had been happening for months and that his behavior worsened, especially when he was under the influence of marijuana and alcohol. Something as simple as my gaze or politely smiling at anyone seemed to trigger him. I've noticed the smell of marijuana anywhere triggers memories of my trauma and abuse. I never saw the abuse for what it was and later I felt so dumb for allowing him to treat me that way and for believing that he even cared for me.

Being true friends, my girlfriends threatened to tell my mom everything if I got back together with Matt. I still loved him and didn't want her to talk me into filing charges, so I never told her. Looking back, I wish I had reported him to make sure that he didn't get away with doing the same thing to another person; I'll never really know…

I remember a cousin's conversation with a friend, *"A man who hits you doesn't respect you."* Those words stayed in my head when my ex called and tried to get back together. I think about those words of wisdom, often.

The advice I have for women going through an abusive relationship is to run, leave and do not look back! Don't allow abuse to happen to you. There is a higher power, and you are here for a reason. *You deserve more, you deserve better, and you deserve nothing less.*

I have healed with faith and serving others, which is what keeps me healing. The advice I have for women in a romantic relationship is to not allow your partner to hit you, it does not matter if it's playful, you are just opening the door to abuse.

I have overcome what could have dragged me down. My life now is so blessed. I am glad to be a part of *Angels of Love*, and to be a voice for women and young girls to know that there is a light at the end of the tunnel. That each woman is far more precious than rubies or diamonds.

What's next for me? I'll go where the wind takes me and do what I need to do. I was a young and naïve "little girl" during the abuse, and I thought this "little boy" was acting like a wannabe man but, a real man would not hit a woman. I was insecure, lacking confidence, and believed I was *nothing* and a nobody. If I could go back and speak to my younger self, I'd tell her that she deserves better.

My hopes and dreams are to help young women who have gone through similar situations and let them know that they are worth it. It's important to remember to let our light shine showing that we are worthy of everything that God says we are.

---My VICTORY Statement---

I have overcome what could have dragged me down. My life now is so blessed. I am glad to be a part of *Angels of Love*, and to be a voice for women and young girls to know that there is a light at the end of the tunnel.

---Chelsea---

MAYRA'S Story...

$\mathcal{I}$ *grew up in San Luis Potosi,* Mexico where I lived with my mother, a brother and sister. My parents separated early, and when I was fifteen years old my mother passed away, and I went to live with my grandparents.

My parents were a traditional and strict family. I wanted to go to work and attend school, but they would ask me why, if all I was meant to do was stay at home, do housework and be a wife? ¿Por qué, si todo lo que se suponía que debía hacer era quedarme en casa, hacer las tareas domésticas y ser una esposa? By this time, I was seventeen years old and felt I never had a parental figure in my life, so I left my grandparents' house to move in with a friend nearby.

For some reason, I was always getting sick, but luckily, my father found out where I was and asked me to live with him, his wife, and my half-siblings in the United States. It felt weird, I hardly knew him since he left me and my family when I was very young. Even though he had tried to reach out to me I had deep resentment towards him. All my life he had more contact with my older brothers than he did with me. I felt he favored them over me.

I explained to my dad what was going on with my relationship with my ex-girlfriend. I was just twenty years old when I met her through a friend's cousin. She was twenty-five years old and lived in the house across the street. She seemed nice enough.

One day, I needed a ride to my house, and she had come along; later she asked my friend for my telephone number. Not too long after that she contacted me about lending her $50 and I told her I could only lend her $20. She knew where I lived and came to pick up the money. That was the moment when she tried to kiss me, but I turned away. We didn't have contact with each other for a long while after that.

I'm a huge soccer fan and I joined a Women's soccer team that my friend's dad formed; it turns out that my ex joined, too. By that time, I had moved out of my dad's house and since I didn't have a car, she would pick me up and drop me off for soccer practice. It was then we started to get closer.

Suddenly, she came back into my life. We communicated more, eager to respond on Facebook messages and texts. It made us feel connected. She was showing more interest and wanting to entice me with dinners and movie dates. At first, I was trying to be careful and go slow with the relationship, but we seemed to really enjoy each other's company; it felt so real. It was romantic and lovely. I had quickly fallen for her.

Before we knew it, I was sharing my life story with her. Right or wrong, my ex-wife was aware of everything that hurt me, and how I tried to overcome the pain. More than anything she knew about the abandonment issues I felt about my father, and how I lived with my mother's absence since she was always working to support me and my siblings, and then her passing away. My ex also knew about the family "secrets," and all the trauma I had gone through in my childhood.

It turns out I was my ex's first girlfriend to meet her parents; unfortunately, her family didn't accept me at first. Worse, they were all out of control drinkers and fights would always break out. It didn't help that I wasn't accepted by her mother, in particular, which was causing a new set of arguments.

My ex was so upset by the rejection that she decided to stay away from her family. The downside was that the anger and stress caused her to start drinking again. She soon blamed me saying that it was my fault that her family wouldn't talk to her and now felt she had no one.

After a while we calmed down with the blaming and officially started dating in January 2014. She had a seven-year-old son, who spent a lot of time with me while she worked, which she did a lot. I would help him with his homework and make something to eat when he asked; I even helped him with his chores. It was a way to bond with him; especially since his mom was gone so much. But it started to feel like they were trying to trap me into their lives. Unfortunately, it didn't take long for her to return to her binge drinking, repeating the dangerous patterns, again.

She started to isolate me from my closest friends and family by saying mean things about them and trying to make me believe that they were using me. She tried to make me see her as the only one looking out for me; that no one would ever love nor respect me more than she did. Yet, she was the one who eventually told me that no one would love me being that I was fat. I had to be careful not to fall for everything she said. She was very manipulative.

What was weird is that I never met any of her friends. It seemed that we would only hang out with my group of friends. It wasn't until she started working at a new job that she finally introduced me to some. My ex was outgoing, the "life of the party" but would always get so drunk that it made her aggressive and argumentative; she lost a lot of friends that way.

One day, a day I wish I could forget, was supposed to be a happy one. It was the night before her birthday. Wanting to surprise her, I took her son with me to buy a cake and presents while she was still at work. Unfortunately, it was late at night, and the surprise was ruined when I opened the door and could tell she was extremely angry and very drunk.

She yelled and asked where I was and why I was out so late with her son. She threw me on to the bed, yelling, pinning me down and calling me horrible names. I tried to explain that we had wanted to surprise her. Hearing that, she got up, and threw the cake on the floor, as she screamed that I was stupid and should have asked.

She started pulling my hair, and pushing me into the bathroom, slamming me against the shower glass door so hard that I closed my eyes terrified that the door was going to break! She wouldn't let go, putting her knuckles with all her force on my cheek but trying not to leave a mark. I'm crying as she then covers my mouth with her other hand telling me not to make any noise because she didn't want to scare her son.

She went on insulting me, cussing and saying horrible things. Her son started crying and came to the bed where I was. She again threw me down, sneering for me to pick up the cake by eating it off the floor.

She started hitting me so hard I was unconscious for a moment. It was past midnight, and I was in panic, I didn't understand what was going on, it was something I had not ever experienced before.

I was trying to leave; she pulled me towards her and tore my blouse trying to make me stay. I made it outside as she came at me, throwing a handful of rocks at my car as I drove away.

I left in total disbelief of what just happened. Still terrified the next day, I refused to answer her calls and texts. She came looking for me asking to forgive her saying that she couldn't remember anything the night before. It was the first time she had ever been aggressive towards me.

As soon as I left, she started making threats over the cellphone. Hours later she texted me asking where I was, that she was waiting for me, and why I left. She said that she loved and missed me, and that it was all a misunderstanding.

I was so confused at what to do so I didn't answer her calls. Later that morning I had a lot of missed calls and messages that said her son was worried about me, about leaving and not saying "goodbye" to him.

Desperate, she told me that she would commit suicide if she had to live without me, and that if anything happened to her, it was going to be my fault. She told me that I would be responsible for taking care of her son, since he already saw me as a mother figure. I was terrified at the thought she would commit suicide, and I would be blamed for it. Worse, the thought of her son having to grow up without a mother like I did, sounded so awful!

I wish I could say it was the last time, but it wasn't. My ex would try to manipulate me by calling me a crazy liar. I don't know why, but after a while I started to believe her. I blamed it on alcohol and begged her to stop drinking. This went on for six long years. I normalized her behavior and began to feel it was my fault for allowing her to treat me so badly.

It began to be the same routine; hit me, offend me, and apologize to me. I only did what she asked because I felt responsible and used to her treatment; it felt familiar.

In the end, I decided to leave her when I found out that she cheated. After leaving, she started to harass me at my job, asking me to try again. The crazy thing is she already had a criminal record for domestic violence made by the person she cheated on me with.

So, my ex tried to be more on the sidelines "waiting it out," so two years passed, we didn't see each other until, one night, at the beginning of May 2015, we went out to a friend's house and had a wonderful time. But she got home and wanted to go to her parent's house around 3am! Being that it was so early, and too far away, I said "No." She began to cry and said that she wanted to see her mom. When I finally asked her if she still wanted me to take her, she suddenly changed her mind, and suspiciously, asked me where I was going, why and who I wanted to go see.

I decided to take her to her mom's after all, but the abuse started again. Insulting me between shouts and punches to my right arm, she then yelled to stop the car. I pulled over and she told me to get out. I barely opened the car door, and she slid over and left me there in the middle of nowhere. I'm without a phone and it's 3-ish in the morning and I was in the middle of nowhere, eight miles from home.

I realized that the relationship has good times and bad. I loved her, I thought she would change, and she promised me that if I married her it was a way for her to show me that she loved me. I would be completely hers, and she, mine.

I was in love and excited for a princess's wedding full of happiness. But my ex-wife told me that we would just go to the courthouse; "If I wanted a princess wedding, I should marry a man" I told her she was who I wanted so we got married on May 6, 2016. It was perfect for a few months. Weekdays seemed to be calm, but weekends were a different story. The hitting started up again; it went on for about 4 years until we separated. She was in jail for abusing another girlfriend. She continues to look for me.

It's not a surprise that I felt like I couldn't trust anyone; even *myself*. I finally looked for help. I found it at *Angels of Love* through their Women's Empowerment program. I learned a lot about myself, and about self-esteem and the importance of having goals. Some of my personal goals are to overcome all the things I have gone through, leaving my fears behind and to learn English better.

I'm happy to say, I now feel calmer with my life. I'm working on my mental health with my dog, Brownie; he's my emotional support dog in every way. He is the reason I get up every morning. I have a stable job working at a snack shop but hope to have a better one in the human service field where I can help others.

What advice would I like to give to women? I would say, to make sure you are taking the time to get to know the person before moving in with them. Leave at any first sight of harm or danger because the situation is *not* going to change or get better, but worse. The longer they abuse you the less they are afraid to hurt you, and the more difficult it is to get out of the relationship. It is also important to know who you are, and how much you are worth because they want to make sure you feel worthless. I want people to know that you must value yourself enough to leave, and that there IS an exit. *Everything passes...Todo Pasa!*

---My VICTORY Statement---

I want people to know that you must value yourself enough to leave,
and that there IS an exit, you need to value yourself enough to leave.
Everything passes...Todo Pasa!

---Mayra---

CINDY'S Story...

I was the youngest of six children and by age nine all my siblings had moved away. I was pretty much left alone. My mother's expectations for her children were for them to leave the house right after high school graduation, regardless of how prepared we were or not. Even though my father was kind, my mom was quite the opposite. She wasn't kind, loving nor nurturing. It could be a reason my parents argued a lot, but, for sure it seemed as though my mom had an issue with me getting close to my father. So, I didn't get affection from either one.

I don't recall mom ever having a meal on the table for us. If I was hungry, I had to wait for her to leave the house to make myself a sandwich and leave just as quickly before she got back. I would have been in deep trouble if she caught me "eating from her groceries". Not only that, one day I got so sick that I called my sister to take me to the doctor because my mom didn't care. As you can see, my basic needs were not met.

Since my mom paid little attention to me, I had a lot of freedom. The greatest part of my childhood was the bond that I had with my friends. We were competitive yet nurtured each other. If I didn't have them, life would have been unbearable. I'm happy to say, I'm still friends with each of them to this day.

I was fourteen years old when I got a shiny, new ten-speed bicycle from my brother. A "teenager with wheels", I became more adventurous! One life-changing night, I rode off to a nearby neighborhood where some of my friends lived. As I was cheerfully pedaling down the street a man I had seen before at the school playground called me over. As I got closer, I could see his eyes were blood shot and I could smell the alcohol on his breath. I told him that I had to go and tried to get back on my bike to leave but he grabbed me, threw me to the ground.

At fourteen, I was raped. I can't remember much of what happened at the time, but I'll never forget after he got up, he told me to just leave. I felt numb and scared as I got onto my bike; it was so painful. In shock, I quietly sobbed as I rode away. One thing I knew was that I could never tell my mom or anyone else about it.

I survived my past and now in my early twenties, I was determined to know love, feel respected and be protected. My best friend had invited me to visit her sister in Hawaii. I was working at a hospital at the time, so I had my own money, and it was a great time to get away. I eagerly said yes! While in Hawaii, I was later introduced to a tourist who eventually became my husband, but there's more to the story, much more…

He was a foreigner, and I've always been attracted to foreign accents. A gentleman, he was everything a girl could dream of; he'd pull out the chair for me and take me out to lavish restaurants. As you know, my home life was dysfunctional; I couldn't wait to grow up and leave the house… so, this was my personal *triumph*!

I remember when I first visited him and his mother in Los Angeles, CA. She would cook amazing meals he specifically wanted. She would immediately make a completely different meal if he didn't like a certain ingredient in a dish. I should have seen the warning signs.

Mesmerized by how close he was to his mother and siblings it didn't matter to me that I couldn't participate in their conversations. I saw their family with rose-colored glasses. I knew I wanted that kind of *stability*; and I wanted that mom figure, that mother-daughter relationship. What

I lacked from my mom was what I was able to get from his mother, and she truly loved me.

Not knowing much about my partner, I learned from his extended relatives that he came from a prominent family and was well-educated. His mom was a beautiful, kind woman, and an excellent homemaker. I eventually lived with them for a few years even though I couldn't speak their language. What I saw in them was *stability*, something I craved. I wanted a real family, regardless of cultural differences.

The first sign of a problem with my partner was that he was a perfectionist. He would say things that would make me feel inferior and humiliated. I didn't clean or cook like his mother, or I didn't do things the way he wanted them to be done were his complaints. I nicknamed him, "Mr. Perfect".

The language barrier started to really affect me emotionally. It was draining, so as a distraction and seeking comradery I quickly found a nursing job and worked the second shift. I was expected to help with the living expenses. I could have had my own place, but I felt the need for love of a family and a mom. I was still hooked by the need for a sense of family *stability*. *Stability* was *so* important to me; it meant trust, safety, and belonging.

After a year's time, I became pregnant. I told him the good news, but he firmly informed me that I wasn't *allowed* to keep the baby. Wanting to confirm that I was indeed pregnant, he took me to a doctor who spoke his language, of course. They talked for a moment, and the doctor instructed me to lie on the table, and before I knew it, I heard a vacuuming sound!

I turned to ask what was going on and the doctor asked me wasn't I there for an abortion, I emphatically said, "No!". I quickly got up as my partner became *livid*. I had never seen him like that, ever. It was frightening. As soon as we got home, he said that I had a choice, I could leave the house or abort the baby and stay.

The next thing I remember is being at the airport. I didn't know where I would go, all I knew was that I dreaded the thought of going to my mother's house, especially pregnant; she was sure to ridicule me. So, I called my sister who lived in the area; she was kind enough to let me stay temporarily with her. I went through my pregnancy without emotional support from my baby's father. I was so, so sad, crying to no end.

It was a difficult delivery, but it helped that my sister was there with me. We welcomed my baby daughter. I called her father throughout the pregnancy; he would never return my calls. I hoped he would come back, but he didn't.

I moved us out of my sister's house into an apartment and found a lady to take care of my daughter while I worked. After her third birthday I finally stopped begging my ex to take us in. Wouldn't you know it, just as I was ready to move on, he called me and told me to come back to Los Angeles. He said that he was arranging our wedding and that there were many gifts waiting for the baby and me. Of course, I was on cloud nine, so I eagerly flew back.

But there were *no* wedding plans, *nor* gifts when we got there. He had lied to me, and I was now stuck. I tried to make the best of it, glad that we were at least together again. After two years of waiting, we finally got married. Four years later I was pregnant with our son; our daughter was now seven years old.

I found out that my ex was cheating with other women, and we had arguments about it, but there was *no* way I was going back home to my mom's. I felt stuck. To make matters worse, he was struggling financially and his mood turned dark; lack of finances triggered him since he was used to "the good life". I decided to keep my distance from him; *Avoidance* was a pattern of mine that I knew all too well. He rejected me, my mom rejected me; rejection and verbal abuse was a shutdown trigger. Mom's belittling "being a mistake" was trauma coming back…

I stayed quiet amongst the confused noise. He portrayed himself as a proper gentleman, very charismatic. However, tired of his womanizing throughout our marriage, I left him but always came back.

With his business affairs bottoming out he decided we should move to his home country. I wouldn't have to work outside of the home, he said. We would have a maid and a driver, he promised. I was expected to only take care of our children. It sounded wonderful, except my co-workers were concerned and told me not to go; but, moving was easy for me, so we left. I've traveled there twice before but visiting and living in a foreign country is completely different, such as not being able to speak or read the language.

Did we have a driver, No, a maid, No. He lied again. Worse, he said I would be able to visit my family in the States but there was a condition...I would *only* be allowed to go, *without* the children. How could I leave without them?!

I found myself deceived again, and captive in a foreign country with very strict cultural norms, including religious exclusions. Basic rights I was used to in the United States, were frowned upon. And to top it off, the language barrier was becoming divisive. My children were learning to speak the language at school and using English less which alienated me even more.

I realized I had to get it together. I started to pick up a little of the language by joining a daily routine with my mother-in-law. We cleaned in the morning and had breakfast after the kids went to school, then walked around the village and had maté tea with some of her elderly neighbors. It was a break from the mundane, but it wasn't enough to feel fully included.

The kids were fine, of course. They were children and felt freer to play outside than they did in LA. After a year I just had to get away; but I didn't know what to do. A day felt like a year. I cried every day. So much so that my mother-in-law told me that I should go into the closet so the neighbors couldn't hear me.

I would often stand by the bedroom window and watch the airplanes fly across the sky praying to God that I'd be on one soon. I was losing my mind, my kids and myself. I was living in a lost, trance-like, going-through-the-motions reality. I felt devastating loneliness.

A few years have gone by, and I'm still stuck there while my ex-husband is working in another country. My marriage was crumbling. We saw him only three or four times throughout the year. I so fervently prayed; and on one miraculous day I met an American lady. We clicked. I told her of my situation, that I *needed* to return to the States. By the grace of God, she knew someone at the American Embassy and told me her friend would contact me. It wasn't long until I received the call and was asked several questions. I was then told that I would need to have someone send money for the airline tickets.

Once the money arrived, I was again contacted by the Embassy. They were ready for us, and *freedom* was finally on its way. I discreetly told my daughter that we were going to leave to the States; she was fourteen. It was mid-May; she begged me to let her finish the school year as it was only two weeks away, but I told her that I couldn't wait, as much as I wished I could. She pleaded that she would beg her dad to let her go after school ended. All I could think of was, I must go *NOW!*

Later that night, while hiding my tears I put together a backpack of clothes for me and my son as discreetly as I could. The next morning, I dropped off my daughter at school, again, trying to be casual, so as to not tip anybody off. Once there, I quietly watched my daughter walk away. I sobbed, my heart, *gutted.*

This is it, it was finally happening; next was the escape plan, the nerve-wrecking drive down the winding mountain to the airport. As described over the phone, I saw the man from the American embassy standing outside the airport entrance. He inconspicuously instructed us to *hurry*. With armed soldiers standing throughout the airport, we quickly followed, praying that we wouldn't get caught. My son and I boarded the plane, and as soon as it took off, I finally gave out a full-bodied sigh of relief and broke down into sobbing tears not caring what anyone thought. All I cared about was that my nightmare was *finally over*!

As soon as we landed, I called my ex-husband telling him that I had left, and that our marriage was over. He was furious that I had left with my son. He fought custody of my son to be returned to his country. I was in the States, and I wasn't afraid anymore. The courts instead allowed him restrictive visitation in a public area whenever he came to America. I informed the school office staff of our situation so that his father could not come by and try to take him.

Knowing my mental health took a beating from childhood up to then, I soon met with a therapist to deal with all the trauma, depression, and anxiety I had experienced. Living with fear has controlled my daily existence. Sadness accompanied me everywhere I went. I was free from my situation, but I couldn't escape my emotional unrest.

The healing journey never ends. I had to rebuild myself emotionally, spiritually, physically, and financially. As a nurse I knew what I had to do to become healthy.

Empowering myself through God's promises was now crucial; I am still a work-in-progress. Today, I serve in the Women's Ministry at my church. I want to give God all the Glory for everything He has brought me out of; trust God and hold on to His promises.

I had been a volunteer for several years with *Angels of Love* and now serve on the Board of Directors. I've introduced my stepdaughters to *Angels of Love's Expect Respect* Teen program. They are now more aware of their potential and expectations. We continue to grow and share with others.

What advice would I give to someone about dating or marriage? I highly advise taking your time to get to know the person. Find out what kind of relationship they have with their parents, family members, and friends. What was their childhood like? Observe their temperament and triggers; are they controlling or jealous? Remember too, looks can be deceiving; sometimes, *dangerously* so.

An extremely important tip from my personal experience for anyone *presently* in an emotionally abusive situation is to have an escape plan. Be very strategic and quiet about your getaway; it's not going to be easy, but staying in a controlling relationship will be much more difficult.

My life now? I'm in a good place where I am happily remarried to a supportive man; and have three stepchildren who love and respect me. I am constantly working on myself and because of *Angels of Love's* Empowerment and Financial Literacy classes, and surrounding myself with good women, I am now in a *stable* place in my life.

With all the education and training, I was able to raise my credit score rating from *Poor to Excellent*; yes, much like my new and improved reality! I'm getting to where I want to be, everything that my ex told me that I couldn't do, I have proven myself capable many times over. I even went to culinary school at South Texas College and I'm proud to say that I'm a great cook now.

A most treasured gift is having my stepchildren tell me that I am a *good* mother, which is what I've always wanted. As the wise Maya Angelou said, *"When we know better, we do better."* is so true. I have come to realize that all I needed was to believe in myself. *Never*, let anyone's opinion define you.

To give back I became a Board member for *The Salvation Army* organization because of everything they did for me when I was young girl. I would go there knowing that I would be fed a hot meal and learn Bible verses. Better yet, when we memorized the verse, we would get cookies; so, I made sure to memorize them all! I now volunteer with them because they were a major source of Agape love and great kindness to me when I needed it most.

There is so much more to my story that my biggest goal now is to write and publish my journey. I hope to turn it into a made-for-tv mini-series to share hope and redemption. Please know, there are resources out there which can guide you to programs for continued education, job training, and a fresh start in life for yourself and your children. In closing this chapter of my life and moving forward, I say to you, *Pray. Believe. Heal. We are not perfect, but* **Worthy.**

---My VICTORY Statement—

Pray. Believe. Heal.
We are not perfect, but **Worthy**.

---Cindy Cavazos---

SARAH'S Story...

I saw the bridge ahead as I stumbled away from the dusty pickup truck. Wait, what's happening?!

The weight of my realization settles like a granite boulder on my chest. I can't quite believe it. Did he really let me just walk away?! Fear again wraps its gnarly fingers around me. The urge to cry is practically begging for its moment.

But I'm not about to give in to that satisfaction. Tears might be cathartic for some, but I marched on, stone-faced and resolute. Bruised inside and out, I shuffled past some boys.

One foot in front of the other, I trudged across that bridge with my head down. My face, sporting more colors than a Picasso painting...blues and purples, that perfect shade of black-and-blue.

The boys gave me a once-over look and mumbled words I couldn't catch; surely, shocked to see someone boldly walking whilst bruised. I can't blame them for being confused.

They moved aside a little, a bit leery. But I keep walking. I'm not looking for sympathy. I'm looking for a way out and I'm taking it. One step at a time, blackened face and swollen, and all.

So, here's to having crossed that bridge, not just from one place to another, but from a life of shadows to one where there's a bit of sunshine awaiting.

Teen years, a time of boundless rebellion and a special kind of invincibility that only youth can bring. Oh, let us not forget the background soundtrack of my mother's words echoing in my ears, like a catchy tune I can't seem to get out of my head. There it is, my mother's voice, not cheering me on but diagnosing my "problem". According to her, my persona was too strong. *Thanks, Mom* for pinpointing the root cause of my life's issues... too much strength, what a *burden* to bear.

Years later, contemplating how I ended up in a marriage that was hastily written like a plot-twist in a bad rom-com. All the while, remembering the waving red flags cautioning me to slow the heck down. But here I am, bumbling through the minefield of false love.

Why dig into the past and bring up skeletons that reside there, you ask? Let me be clear, I do not want your pity. Trust me, feeling sorry for me would be like adding an extra layer of embarrassment. It's often said that life's lessons are meant to be shared. Somewhere along the lines, I got caught-up in a whirlpool of misleading emotions, false promises, and child-like naiveté.

And, as for failing my mother and myself...we all take detours in life, some scenic routes that we later regret, but maybe...just maybe, this bridge I'm walking isn't just a path of reflection, but a stepping-stone to something greater.

The strongest stance I can take is to acknowledge the past and my missteps while moving forward to be a beacon of wisdom for the masses, or to remind us that strength comes in many forms. Whether we fall, falter or fly, we are still moving forward, and that's where the real story lies.

Many years removed, I find myself upon the bridge of retrospection; contemplating the twists and turns that led me into such a marriage...

again, recalling those vivid red flags fluttering in dire warning, urging me to halt in my tracks but, I blatantly ignore them.

Recent brooding prompted me to explore the intricacies of *why* we often choose to remain ensnared within relationships that are clearly detrimental. It brought up a buried memory that unveiled the seeds of this conviction, a memory that traces back to my tender years of age six. A little girl who reveled in dresses, donning on white shoes adorned with delicate lace... A teacher's pet, I unabashedly embraced my love for learning.

Emerged in a stark incident of the memory of a boy relentlessly reaching out to touch my hair. Distressed and repelled by his unwelcomed advances, my pleas to the teacher fell on deaf ears. Undeterred by my vocal protests, he continued his pursuit without consequence.

With unwavering resolve, I abandoned my instinct to flee and instead embraced defiance. Armed with a rock, propelled by a well sprung pent-up frustration, I launched it at him with all my might. He never pursued me again; for me, the problem was solved. However, addressing the evident mixture of care and confusion, my mother reasoned that his persistent attention was his expression of fondness for me. I retreated to the family car in tears with unvoiced questions and misunderstood emotions.

Amidst the jungle of said emotions and questions that lingered from that encounter, I embarked on a journey of self-exploration, and illuminating the "why's" of choices I would unknowingly make in the realm of relationships.

Thus, intertwined with the very fibers of my understanding of perfection, boundaries, and self-worth. Just as I had misconstrued his advances as a twisted expression of affection, I found myself drawn to partners who mirrored this pattern. Misguided, I interpreted over-stepped boundaries as displays of love.

The cycle was familiar, almost comforting in its familiarity. And, here I now stand, recognizing the intricate threads connecting my past to my present. My understanding of that young girl's actions was to safeguard her boundaries and demand respect.

Armed with this newfound insight, it stands as a cornerstone in the edifice of my resilience, a testament to the strength that has always resided within me. The path ahead is revealed by the glow of attuned discovery, and the healing commenced with every stride.

There I am, walking across the bridge with each stride I take...my journey unravels with drama, flare, and spontaneous moments of clarification. As I walked, I shed layers of uncertainty, regret and self-doubt that once weighed me down. Strutting through the remnants of my fears with deliberate choice to leave behind the patterns that no longer served me and embracing the unfiltered narrative of my life.

With each step, I am not just moving from one side to the other...I'm stepping over into a new scene...a new chapter... and maybe, yes, maybe, a new version of myself.

My mother, the roaring hurricane of a life coach, had yet met her match in me, the self-proclaimed unstoppable force. So, there I am, a teenager, a romantic but oh-so-green in the game of love. My father, the Master of Authority. Poor lads who were interested in me but weren't worth my time if they couldn't chat about *theology* according to Dad. I was nineteen and flailing in the sea of inexperience, desperate to rebel against anything remotely resembling authority. I was twenty-seven years old when I married the one who made my heart race and mind spin, all in less than *two months*! I could go on!

But, back to that fateful night when my life took an unimaginable shift. There I was, stripped down, physically, and emotionally by a man I barely recognized anymore. I'm handcuffed. I could see the border bridge through a gap of the smelly blanket that was thrown on top of me. Fear was becoming a reality. He was crossing the border and driving me into Mexico; I was being kidnapped… TAKEN. Those razor blades… were they meant for me!? Who will *ever* find me now?! Will I ever be *found*?!

Stripped of my dignity, I faced an unspeakable violation as I'm subjected to assaults more than once within the confines of this dusty vehicle. My body bore the weight of the trauma while tightly bound at my hands, all the while positioned horizontally across the rear seat floor. Veiled by darkness, my cries for help silenced by the expanse around me. My mouth gagged and covered with a thick strip of silver tape, but that did not stop me…not a chance! Not a chance, because fear can't silence a headstrong spirit, especially one that's hell-bent on survival…even when shackled and terrified.

My mouth taped shut but my spirit was not bound. Saliva became my weapon; slowly, painstakingly slow, the tape began to loosen; it gave way, the rag fell out of my mouth as a muffled sob of triumph and resilience filled the air.

My mother didn't raise me to be a victim! My head-strong spirit was more than just bravado…it was a lifeline, a reminder that even in the darkest moments I could rise above it!

So, there you have it, a snapshot of a terrifying night that defied all odds, where my fear met with my determination head-on because strength isn't always about muscle force, it's about the unwavering resolve that courses through your veins, the fire in your heart that refuses to be extinguished. Here's to bridges crossed, to battles fought, and to a realization that even in the most harrowing of moments, strength can shine through and the impossible can become possible. Imagine this, a patchwork of swollen bruises as I stepped onto that bridge. The journey across that bridge isn't just a walk… it's a *march* towards redemption.

As I approached the U.S. border sign, the authorities awaited. I have nothing… no I.D., no documents to prove who I am. My face battered; stripped down, and wearing his oversized jacket were the first things they saw; but within, there was a Warrior, it was the embodiment of both my trauma and my strength.

This person walking, she's more than just a fellow captive…she's a sister-in-struggle. She too knows the darkness that only captivity can bring. She'd been bound, violated, and abused, but her spirit wasn't shattered; instead, she clung to her faith, whispered prayers to Jehovah God, begging for strength beyond her own. In her vulnerability, she found unexpected power----"Speak for me—only you have the power!" her heart cried out, as she relied on faith to be her voice when she had none left.

Back in the unforgiving Mexican terrain under a tree; with no rights, no identification and in the face of hopelessness, that steadfast faith remained unshaken. Amid this turmoil, I summoned the wellspring of her innerspring, even as his blood mingled with mine. Yes, he had inflicted wounds upon himself; bleeding out from his wrists…his blood pouring over me. I chose to grasp onto his humanity to expose his vulnerability.

I recognize that my survival hinged on saving him as well. So, I embraced him, letting him pour out his tears over me. Waiting for it to reach a moment of calm, where he could truly see me, not just as a captive, but as the mother of his child and a woman who had once been a significant part of his tumultuous life.

When I first encountered him, my first husband, he concealed his marital status. The two-month whirlwind of romance that I allowed myself to be swept under didn't give me time to learn more about him. Astonishingly, he fathered five children with five different women and had gone through four marriages' prior… all ending in divorce due to *violence*, on his part. To all the women out there, taking a closer look and seeking protection is *paramount*. Investigate, inquire, and safeguard yourselves, it is a crucial step that should never be overlooked.

Flashback to our love story…*the "happy times"*…we were married for four years. It was a romance built on the unstable foundation of emotions running wild. I even named our children based on various emotions I experienced.

And now, I am at the intersection of recounting a tale for you. I want to tell you and remind everyone that I am not a victim. There is no sugarcoating the dark chapters. I did not come out of that tornado, broken nor defeated. I came out strong, and strong is an understatement.

I'm crossing the threshold from *victim* to *survivor*. We all find ourselves in relationships for reasons that are complex. We stayed, not just because of love, but because of fear, entanglement, and the unrelenting desire to fix what's broken. We're terrified, terrified of failing and admitting defeat in a world that often judges us by the success of our relationships. We're entangled in the web of family heritage and societal expectations.

As women, we carry a unique burden like an unspoken legacy. We're taught to be strong, to persevere, and to hold our families together at all costs. We are Warriors on the surface, but sometimes, that strength becomes our iron cage, trapping us in situations we're too afraid to escape from.

I recall the numerous attempts I made to break free, striving to escape the abusive emotional chains. "…your reasons are *insufficie*nt!", they declared. My own family, who were supposed to shield and support me, uttered these words. They invalidated my experiences by casting a shadow of doubt over the very emotions that should have warranted empathy. How many of us have stood in the same bleak corner with voices stifled by shame, fear, and guilt?

The truth we present, often curated and carefully selected fragments of reality that hardly scratch the surface of what lies beneath. I know that countless other women are out there right now wrestling with the same demons. They're living in the shadows of their own lives, haunted by the ghosts of their choices, and shackled by the weight of their history.

We need to shine the light on these stories, on the silent battles that rage within us. By sharing our stories by speaking up we break the cycle of silence. We're giving permission to other women, other survivors to find their own strength and their own path to liberation.

So, yes, it's uncomfortable. Yes, it's exposing the raw underbelly of our lives...but it's also about *redemption*, about turning our *pain* into a source of *power*.

Refuse to be silent, no longer defined by the scars we wear. In sharing, we're creating a community of strength, a sisterhood of survivors, and a legacy of resilience.

I'm here because I want to shout from the rooftops that despite our strength, despite our determination, we are all vulnerable when it comes to matters of the heart. It is okay.

I have three daughters. Each is unique in their strength and softness at heart. I've whispered to them, *"Be kind but be strong."* It's about striking a balance...about teaching them that while fairytales have their place, real love takes work...it's about communication, compromise, and commitment.

Above all else, I want my daughters to know that being strong means having the courage to show vulnerability but also to write their own endings and shape their own futures with the strength within.

Now, let me share a glimpse of my new husband, Marty; a man of patience and devout faith, a family man guided by his unwavering belief in God, stands with the strength of a lion and the patience of Job. His steadfast presence alongside me truly deserves recognition.

If anyone merits a Nobel Peace Prize, it is he, but wait... I'm the *Grand Prize*!

---My *VICTORY* Statement---

...my fear met my determination head-on because strength isn't always about muscle force, it's about the unwavering resolve that courses through your veins, the fire in your heart that refuses to be extinguished.

---Sarah Sagredo-Hammond---

Would you like to read my full unedited story?
Please go to @sarah_atlasrgv
I'd like to share with you my previously published
poem Foxy Phoenix.

FOXY PHOENIX

By Sarah Hammond

As a child I felt I was a blossom, an unbroken gift,

They ask, how did I change, what made me become?

I respond, "I burned to ash so someone else could see.

What they could make of me;"

Would I stand tall, would I fall and bleed

How much of myself would I concede?

I fell, BUT I became ME.

A woman, tall and proud, a woman smart and strong.

A woman without a doubt.

A Phoenix, fire and strength inside her heart.

I tell my daughters, "Burn baby burn, rise above the coal."

Be kind. Be strong. Above it all,

Burn and stand, never fear a fall. ©

CLAUDIA'S Story...

My story begins when I was in high school. I met my first ex-husband at a party my brother held at our home. He came over with a cousin of mine and hung out for the whole weekend. He was very, very jealous, and would even stalk me at school. He hated when I would hang-out with my friends or talk to guys, in general. Well, I ended up getting pregnant. My parents were furious and adamant that I had to move out. We were forced to get married, it was quick, and I had no choice about the matter.

It wasn't too long before I noticed that my ex-husband and I were not in a good place. We had minor arguments at first, but later, it progressed to his being physically abusive towards me. In 1991, our first argument was after bringing home our firstborn son. We got into a heated argument about having to wait on the "40-days" doctor's orders so that my body could heal before we could be intimate again. Another trying time for us was during the wintertime, and he wanted to take our 3-month-old son outside in the cold, to a party, of all things. I worried that my son would catch a cold. My ex was so angry with me that he left the house for the whole weekend.

With the costs of a new baby, we were struggling financially so I found a job at Pizza Hut. One evening, my boss and I were working in the back storage room. My ex-husband showed up unannounced and he watched us walk out from the back together. My ex became spitting mad and rushed outside. My boss's tires had gotten slashed, and I just knew my ex-husband had done it. Though I was so afraid I would lose my job, I confessed to my boss that my ex-husband had more than likely vandalized his car. The police were called and eventually a police report was filed.

I remember we had a huge fight on a particular weekend; it was frightening. We were at my parents' home, in their bedroom, while my sister happened to be visiting. I don't remember what we were fighting about but he was livid. There I was holding my baby as I cried out to my sister to take him so that he wouldn't get hurt in the altercation.

My husband pushed me down on top of the bed, and he got on top of me, his hands around my throat and started choking me. I'm gasping for air. I finally yell out to my sister to call 911 as I'm kicking and fighting him off. I got away and ran outside to my car, but he caught up with me. As I'm trying to drive off he manages to pull me out of the car and bring me down to the ground, the door slams shut, hitting my leg. My head, hitting the concrete driveway with full force.

I was in and out of consciousness, but I remember the sheriff showing up and taking him into custody. As my family rushed over to me, my dad yelled as to why I wouldn't leave him. He's going to kill you, he'd say.

I pressed charges, not once, not twice. Though separated, we ended up talking again and became pregnant with my second son; this was back in 1993. We eventually officially got back together. But it didn't last that long, as the physical abuse continued. I finally decided to file for divorce.

It was 1993, and it was a challenging time in my life; I was so ashamed and overcome with depression. I felt like a failure. I knew I wanted a better life. I wanted change and to get out of this situation for good but didn't know where to start. It was then that I saw a commercial on tv about getting training at a trade school. It was an opportunity to change my life, make a difference, and that's when I decided to work towards a nursing career. I became a CNA, a certified nursing assistant. My life, my children's lives were going to finally change for the better.

My ex-husband wanted to see the boys, so we started talking again, and yes, we ended up getting back together, yet again. And that was when I ended up getting pregnant with my daughter. This is now 1997, I went through a "wild" phase of going out and partying. I realized it was a way for me to numb all the pain that was going on in my life, and in my eyes, the marriage was over.

It turned out I met someone and got married to my second husband. He eventually became my second ex. I found myself in a new battle. He turned out to be an alcoholic. I was now dealing with emotional and verbal abuse. It sounded familiar, as he didn't like me to hang out with friends thinking that it was disrespectful for me to be talking to other men. He was jealous, angry, and controlling.

Life was starting to feel empty and depressing again. My children and I were living in a dysfunctional and chaotic household, and I knew I had to find a way out. I knew I had to go back to school to make a better life for myself, and that I didn't want to rely solely on my husband. I also knew I didn't want him to deter me, so, right or wrong, I planned to go to school behind his back, if I had to.

I had a friend who was in a nursing program, her name was Judy. Judy blessed me in so many ways. She guided me through the nursing program application and registration, for starters. Judy gave me her assigned books and uniforms which saved me from having to buy them. It all became real…I was going back to school, I had no choice but to tell him. He wasn't happy. "No one told you to go back to school. I'm not going to help you. Why can't you be those wives that stay at home?" I knew it wasn't going to be easy, but I had a mission to accomplish my goals. I found myself blessed beyond blessed as God put angels in my life to help navigate through the ups and downs. I was determined to be an overcomer; and I am!

I met my friend Abel at the daycare. He gave me rides to school and took my kids to his daycare that he owned when my car broke down. The nursing program and home life was such a challenge. I was an emotional mess, and my husband was of no help. I found myself in the hospital due to stress and dehydration just trying to balance everything. I remember I was about to have a nervous breakdown. I begged Abel to please open the daycare early so that I could drop off my kids at 5 a.m.

Desperate, I confided in Abel that I was pregnant again and that I needed to make this plan work out. I *need* to finish the semester! His fiancé was aware of my being overwhelmed and needed Abel's help. I remember his answer to my plea was, "Don't worry, we're Christians…we will help you; bring the kids and finish up your schooling." I think about all the things that happened through that year and how my prayers were answered and aligned everything in my path. I just want to bless in abundance everyone who helped. I am so grateful and thankful for their grace and mercy.

When it came to my financial needs, like paying off my school courses, I was exceptionally blessed by my friend Norma who is no longer with us. May she rest in peace; she helped me secure a loan that fully covered my nursing school costs. My nursing career was something that I wanted so badly that I will forever be grateful to my Heavenly Father for blessing me throughout my obstacles, and one thing for sure, I got out stronger through it all. I knew that I would be okay.

I didn't know how I was going to do it but looking back, I couldn't believe what I went through. I remember being very pregnant and praying my baby would *not* be born early as graduation was on November 2, 2000. Our daughter arrived on November 30th! It was surely a year that I will never, ever forget. Just believe that Angels were put in our path so we can finish what we started.

I'd like to say, being part of this collection of stories and sharing this moment with these amazing women who are *overcomers* is a great honor. We proved that we could get out and chase our dreams. At the time, I didn't have the resources that *Angels of Love* now provides the community with a safe place to go to but, I want to say thank you, *Angels of Love* for this momentous honor and opportunity to inspire someone else and say to them, you will be okay and that you can make it through. May God bless you all in abundance.

---My VICTORY Statement---

I knew it wasn't going to be easy, but I had a mission to
accomplish my goals. I found myself blessed beyond blessed as
God put Angels in my life to help navigate through the ups and downs.
I was determined to be an overcomer; I am!

---Claudia Acevedo---

KATHLEEN'S Story...

Although my parents were financially secure, they had a marriage of convenience. It didn't help that my mom was volatile towards my dad. My father was a coach, and my mother was a social worker; both chose their careers over being parents. My mother wouldn't allow my brother and me to have a close relationship with my dad. She also chose to give all her attention and focus to a sister my parents adopted. I was the most ignored.

My parents were divorced by the time I was eleven, and when I was thirteen my mother passed away from stage 4 ovarian cancer. She has been dead for 20 years and I still pray to God for forgiveness towards her and try not to resent her. It has been difficult. I recognize that I've always felt broken due to my childhood. At the same time, though my younger years were unstable and having lost one of my best friends in a car accident when we were both twenty, I loved life and trusted people. I was genuinely a happy person before I met my ex-husband.

My ex and I knew each other from when we attended the same high school for a brief time and later reconnected on social media. When he was sober he was a good guy, but when he was using drugs he was abusive and just a mean, horrible person. As a young woman in my 20's, I believed his lies and honestly thought he would change, get better and sober up.

Like my parents, my ex's parents were also divorced. He had a closer relationship with his dad as his mom was argumentative and would even fight with *us both* causing a bit of a rift in their mother-son relationship, let alone in ours. I feel my ex's parents enabled his behavior which probably bonded them in a weird way. As expected, my ex and his sister had a troubled childhood as I did.

Verbally abusive early in the relationship, my ex blamed it on having PTSD as a veteran. It was about a year and a half into our marriage when he became physically abusive. He slapped and choked me, a fact I'd rather not tell in detail. His addiction was a major factor in the abuse and the break-up of our marriage. His friends were his coworkers, and they seemed nice enough, except for the fact that they were also his drug dealers. It turns out, he was a drug addict *long* before I met him. I was naïve and ignored the red flags.

I would pray to God to take me out of my marriage, somehow. The constant stress caused facial paralysis as my right eye lid wouldn't open on its own. My nerves were beyond shot. I developed anxiety and panic attacks which caused me to wake up in the middle of the night gasping for air. I later developed a severe case of pneumonia and was hospitalized. My ex even left me at the hospital saying he'd be right back but didn't. I later found out that he got high on cocaine and "ice." I felt hopeless, scared, and feared for my future, and my life.

I tried my best to shield my children from his behavior. I'd keep them with me in their bedroom when he was acting erratically, or I slept in the same room to keep an eye on them. When things really got bad, I would take them and leave for the day or go to my aunt's for the weekend, returning only when he left for his work, which was out of town.

He always apologized after hurting me and promised to change, which is why I didn't tell anyone what was going on. I did my best to hide my arms and the body parts that were covered with bruises. I wanted so badly to believe that he would stop. It wasn't until my brother found out that I was in the hospital and told my family that they started asking questions;

I finally told them the truth.

My ex leaving me alone in the hospital and not coming back was a big eye-opener for me. I can honestly say it helped me realize not only my ex-husband's priorities but the degree of his addiction. I could have been *dying*, and he wouldn't have been there for me.

We were always struggling financially, and I got tired of having to hide my wallet and car keys because he would drain our bank account and steal money from me. I hated my life so much and I desperately needed to get away from what was causing it to be so hellish…*him*. I wish I could say that he was gone for good after we separated, but he wasn't.

I established myself by getting an apartment and doing well; so well that he tried several times to come back. Unfortunately, I allowed him to come back for the sake of "family". But things were going to be different this time. Different, as I was now mentally stronger and wouldn't tolerate his abuse.

Sadly, I had realized that I didn't love him anymore, and towards the end I felt like I would rather work three jobs to provide for myself and my children than stay with him. Instead, I enjoyed a stable life with my kids when he wasn't around. It became a *familiar* marriage of convenience. I had just started my first semester back to school after taking a six-year break having to focus on *him and his issues*. I was working a full-time and a part-time job. I was getting stronger mentally and building up courage to permanently leave him.

It wasn't too long before I got to the point of being so annoyed with how much he depended on me that I had had enough. I've never met a more helpless person in my life! I was so tired of how financially unstable he was and how he would lie about money to cover his drug addiction, and anything *else* he was doing behind my back. Everything about him was so *gross* at that point.

To my horror and disgust, I found activity on his phone and caught him engaging in inappropriate behavior. It was a done deal for me, and it was a good thing I had strategically enrolled to finish my bachelor's degree before leaving him. I immediately filed for divorce.

After taking *Angels of Love*'s Empowerment classes and counseling sessions I'm happy to say I started to thrive. I'm still working at the same company years later. One month after my divorce, I was approved for a house loan and within six months became a homeowner. I'm proud to say, I earned a master's degree and had set in motion my success before I left him. *"Where there's a will, there is a way."* As the old saying says.

Things I'm going through at this stage? I still have trouble letting my walls down and haven't learned to trust a man, yet. I truly can't imagine finding someone who will love and treat me well. But I hope one day I can have a healthy and loving marriage. Also, I have had nightmares for years due to the abuse, so I may start therapy to help change my mind-set. Yes, I am still trying to heal, but the stable and normal life I have built for my children brings me peace. I'm satisfied with my career and accomplishments for now.

Were there signs that I now realize as red flag behaviors? Yes, there were times my ex would leave the room to go to the restroom every 10 minutes… always saying, "I'll be right back". Doing that made things so noticeable.

My advice to anyone dealing with domestic violence is to know and not ignore red flags, to not tolerate any type of abuse, whether mentally or physically. If the relationship is a challenge in the beginning, leave. Nothing should ever be so hard to make work. No matter how scary it may be to start over, being safe is far better than wasting or fearing your life.

The purpose of sharing my story is to let others who may be struggling know that there is light at the end of the tunnel after you leave. You *can* be ok. You will become financially stable and successful *if* you work toward your goals. You can accomplish anything you set your mind to and make your dreams come true. After my divorce I bought my home, graduated with my bachelor's and then, a master's degree. My children are healthy and whole. I live in peace. If I could do it so can anyone who might feel they can't.

It might be controversial to say this, but please allow me, it's important to understand that everyone has a story, including the person who hurts us. Whether parent, spouse or otherwise, their harm against us is wrong, and *never* justifiable; but to fully heal one has to have some sense of understanding, and yes, compassion for that person, at some point.

How is my life now? I'm not completely healed from the trauma as healing is a process, but I have faith that one day I will be. I enjoy not fearing for my safety.

I am very proud of the stable life my children have because of me; hence, I have shared with you *only* a small window of my life as a victim of abuse.

Thank you for understanding the need for some privacy, especially for my children's sake, and respect to him and his family even if I may not have been given such. On that note, I focus on my responsibilities as a mother and take pride in their successes and in my giving them the best life possible. I am happy to say that I am not the same person I was…I am stronger and hopeful.

---My *VICTORY* Statement---

I focus on my responsibilities as a mother and take pride in their successes and my giving them the best life possible. I am not the same person I was…

I am stronger and hopeful.

---Kathleen Barras---

CELESTE'S Story...

If I stood before you right now, you would have no idea what I have risen from. One would see in front of them a confident, high-energy, classy entrepreneur with a million-dollar smile. Yes, that spark is who I was always meant to be, and a reminder of the seed I am. Like many seeds, I have endured both flourishing and withering times. Our character is often molded by our experiences, and this is mine.

My parents married very young, and though very much in love, that quickly decayed along with a trail of misery, infidelity, and abuse. My siblings and I were witnesses to many arguments that often escalated to full-on battery and assault. It wasn't long before they divorced, and my dysfunctional family was fractured. I was sent to live with my grandmother, and my brothers were sent to my father. As you can imagine, my early years of growing up had been tainted with trauma, abuse, and unspeakable extremes that no child should ever go through in life. Thank God for my grandmother and her saving grace.

My mom eventually remarried and started a new second family, as did my father. My brothers and I grew up rarely seeing each other, besides the occasional custody plots my mother schemed, but that is for another story. Being raised by my grandmother was perfect; I was safe and loved. Most of the time, it felt like I was an only child. She instilled in me the values and determination I lead by, and I credit the woman I am today to her. Her raising me was not easy, there was a rough brief period where we were homeless due to my grandmother losing her job.

We were living in a van, showering in the morning at a relative's home, attending school during the day while she went looking for a job, and sleeping on cold nights in a hospital parking lot. This time taught me that even though one can fall on hard times, you must always keep pushing forward and never give up on yourself. I apply this rule daily in my business and personal life. She quickly got back on her feet and provided a more than perfect lifestyle for a young girl. I will be forever grateful to my *Shero* for taking me in and loving me as her daughter.

At age 14, my mom got "a wild hair" and decided she wanted me to live with her, and by this time, I had a trust fund with substantial money secured for my future. Against my will, she forced legal action, and I was ordered to live with her, my stepdad, and half siblings. Living with them was a huge adjustment, though I did love my siblings, this new environment came with a lot of conditions, arguments, and having to deal with a mother who was absent for most of my life. My mom and I could not get along, and most of our disputes turned into arguments that often escalated to fights.

I recall this as a dark time in my life where I was depressed but could never show it to the world and kept that spirit and determination. I would tell myself, *you're almost an adult and will walk away from this.* Having great friends and spending summers with my grandmother was my refuge, and it got me through it. At age 16, I landed my first real part-time job in sales and loved every minute of it. I could now provide for myself in many ways, but it was also when life began to shift, again.

The summer before I turned 17, my mom, stepdad, and half-siblings moved away to another town without taking me, nor my final year of high school into consideration. I was told that I was moving back to live with my grandmother. No plan in place for how I was to finish my year or what my future held; I was dropped like a sack of potatoes. I didn't care; I was back with my grandmother.

I was ambitious and knew I was at my last hurdle, and then I could finally start my life. My goal was to attend college in New York, so I applied and waited to hear back. During this time, I met a boy through a mutual friend, and we started chatting online. I found him charming, respectful, funny, and our connection was instant.

Danny told me he was a 20-year-old accounting college student and I shared that I was a 17-year-old high school student. We quickly fell head over heels for each other and began dating. Our love began as all do, he was my knight in shining armor, and I was his All-American girl, we shared with each other our hopes and dreams. We continued to fall madly in love with each other. He ended up coaxing me to sleep with him, to which I did.

"The letter" finally arrived, and I was accepted to the college of my dreams! My life was almost at the finish line. I begin to set up my affairs and plan for my move, only to get the most heart-wrenching news, my nest egg has dwindled down to almost nothing. To clarify what I had been preaching to my attorneys all along, only to be told I was a child and could not comprehend the matter. I will not mention any names of any of the parties involved, but you know who you are. My dream was crushed, and now I had to change course again.

Due to this financial issue, the repercussions changed my whole life, all in one day. I left home, moved into a hotel, and ceased communication with my family, leaving me to depend on my boyfriend. A teen with a few thousand dollars on hand led to some *big girl* decisions quickly; they were not all the best decisions but did what I had to do at that time.

My boyfriend was very supportive at this time, and since I was a minor, a lot was placed under his name: my hotel reservations, a new vehicle, and he even convinced me to hand over all my cash for him to hold so it won't get stolen. I continued to attend school, work two jobs, and live in hotel rooms. With no stable place to live, I continued to move and pay for hotels, as the money dwindled down, so did the motels. But, I was finally free and in love, what more could a girl ask for?!

During our time of courtship, he would speak of an ex-girlfriend who hadn't gotten over him. There were multiple encounters where she would cause a scene, but I never met her and just wrote it off to what I was told. The incidents became more frequent, so I began to doubt he was telling me the truth.

One time while driving down the expressway, I began to question him intensely about this woman, and it escalated to an argument that ended with him throwing a punch that landed on my forehead. In utter shock, I continued to drive, and he quickly apologized but blamed me for his action and losing control. My forehead swelled, and I quickly began to conceal the bruising with makeup. I accepted his apology and shortly after this incident, the ex-girlfriend and I had a face-to-face encounter.

This led to the truth being exposed, and in fact, she was *still* his girlfriend! Again, how this unfolded is for another story, but to make a long story short; he once again asked for forgiveness to which I again forgave him, believing with all my heart that we were meant to be together. To show how committed he was to our relationship, he asked me to move into his parent's house with him, and I agreed.

While living together, we spoke about starting a family and being young parents; it was not long after turning 18, I became pregnant. While finding out the great news, we immediately ran off to the courthouse and got married. During this time, some disturbing truths came to light; he had lied about his age *and* real name. He was, in fact, seven years older than I was!

It gets better, the name he gave was not even a middle name, but a *nickname* that he chose for himself after the great professional football player, "Dan Marino"! I didn't realize at the time, but he deliberately targeted me when I was underage, and though I didn't know the term "grooming" at the time, I now understand precisely what it is and its evilness to prey on young girls and boys. As the story goes, I am now his 18-year-old pregnant wife.

Working multiple jobs to support my family and living with him under his parents' roof I began to settle into my new role. My focus became the baby and our family. One day I came home for lunch to find evidence of him having had sex with another woman in the house. When I confronted him, he beat me and dragged me throughout the house.

I fought back or tried to free myself using my nails, hands, legs, anything I could do to escape, but he was stronger. The police were called, and I was taken to the Emergency Room, and he was hauled to jail. At the Emergency Room, I dreaded the call I had to make, but with no one else to turn to, I called my mom. It had been a while since we had really spoken, and I had to let her know what was going on.

She arrived at the hospital, and I began to explain everything. Thinking that she is a survivor of domestic abuse, and my mother that she would intervene and remove me from the dangerous and inappropriate situation; instead, she does the *unthinkable*.

Upon my discharge from the hospital, she dropped me back off at *his* home. She tells me, "Women, get beat up by men. That is what men do. Men are allowed to be aggressive with women and that is how it's been forever." Basically saying, *"deal with it"*. She leaves me there and goes to help get my husband out of jail. This is the point where I realize, I am utterly *alone!*

Thinking about my unborn baby and the future, I sought help from a local shelter the next day, only to be told they couldn't help. I reached out to friends who offered a place to stay but learned quickly that I didn't have enough to make ends meet. Eighteen and pregnant, nowhere to go was now even darker than it had been a few years earlier. I had to accept his apology and make this marriage work.

Our son was born in the Spring, and for the next few years, our marriage juggled from happy to turbulent times, leading to separation. We spent our lives in a violent environment, isolated, with his infidelity spiraling, always parting and returning to one another with hopes to salvage our marriage for our son. Our fights became more aggressive, physical and to the point that objects were being used. About this time, the fights were so frequent, his vice of choice was taking blows to my head, pulling my hair, and I had to defend myself causing scratches on him. This often resulted in my being arrested and taken to jail.

I lost faith in the police department right about the time a cop told me I probably deserved to be beaten, and another asked me to sleep with him. They saw me as a young, troubled girl, labeling and calling me a statistic, never a person. The case would get tossed but the unfair cycle continued. Our son witnessed these altercations and was dragged back and forth from home-to-home during the times of separation. No mother would want this life for their child. I endured, prayed, and stayed with the hope that this would all end one day. I hoped he would change.

After three years, I finally filed for divorce, but this only made matters worse. My grandfather had just passed and recalled him being the one who stood up for me and told him to never let him lay a hand on me again, and to always fight back. His words were more colorful and passionate, but his wisdom and acceptance gave me the strength I needed.

This time my ex was caught in an affair, while our son had been admitted to the hospital. His lies had unraveled far enough; I was done. It was time to end it once and for all. Boy, was I wrong! This just fueled him into a monster with the sole purpose of destroying my life at all costs.

While waiting for the divorce to be finalized, I had not considered the proximity of my home. I had built my first house while we were separated. It was an ideal time to be less than five minutes away from his parents' home, and later my brother-in-law and his family became my next-door neighbors.

Why is this important? Guess who started to come around at all hours during the day and night. You guessed it. Mind you, he was not coming to see our child but to check in and see what his wife was up to. I would ask him to leave, but he would refuse; and if the cops got involved, he would just jump next door. Stalking began, harassment was endless, and he then began sleeping with women I thought were my friends, only to gather intel about me.

Finally, the divorce was granted, and I was free. This was not how I pictured my life, but now I could forge my new path for my son and me. At this point, he stepped away from our son's life and became this psychopath with laser-focus on me. Thank God for my friends and their support as this went from bad to worse for almost a decade.

My life became an eternity of one big endless nightmare. At some point, it was so unbearable and exhausting that I would call his bluff and return to him, just to make our "family work." These times served as a quick blip in time. It always resulted in the same insanity as before the divorce: the lying, the cheating, the fighting, physical and emotional altercation escalating, and the trust was forever broken, but I can always say, *I tried*.

I once came home from a work trip to find my ex had broken in and stolen property, yet the cops did nothing. Ultimately, I ended up losing the home due to these recurring episodes becoming unbearable to continue living there. I decided to move to a town away, and he begged for one last chance. We again moved in together, to only end up with the same result.

The great Albert Einstein once said, "The definition of Insanity is: doing the same thing over and over again and expecting different results." That was me. The cycle continued, and the hell was intense; but I continued to lean on my friends, family, and faith to move past this. My son was my life, my reason, and with a whole lot of prayer, running away, moving from place to place, all the while enduring his hell, my life continued.

He eventually got a girl pregnant and married her, it is one of the most *fabulous* days of my life! He would have no choice but to leave me alone. However, that was not the case; he continued, but in respect for my son and his wife, I have left out the details. My ex's wrath continued, but I held my ground and vouched to tell his wife if he continued to bother me. The random late-night calls of silence continued, unexpected gifts delivered to my door unaccepted. Finally, it was my turn to gain *my* power back.

I met my new husband around this time, and he was able to experience some of these incidents; he was quick to put his foot down and intervened. This seemed to calm him a bit, not without some back-ended comments; but for the most part, I was seeing light at the end of the tunnel.

Today, I am a successful small business owner, who is happily married to the man who stood up to my punisher. We have since added to our family three more beautiful children, three dogs, and a life of devotion to our children, faith and community.

How I survived all this and lived to tell the story is a question that haunts and fuels me today! Years of suffering from a childhood of hardship, straight into adulthood still baffle me today. I have since become an advocate for women and children and have pleaded to our legislators to act, make change, and implement laws to end abuse and protect survivors.

Law enforcement needs to be more educated, proactive, and vigilant. You will catch me often in my talks stressing that we women were considered property from biblical times till the 1980s. Laws had been set in place, where a husband could rape and assault his wife, and it was legal! It's time to stand up, speak up, and seek justice for all women who have been in my situation, and for those who lost their lives in the hands of their abusers. It's time to face reality and break the cycle of abuse. Let's rise and stand for women. Our voices will be heard!

Agencies like *Angels of Love* are beacons of hope and resources. I truly wish they were around when my nightmare started. I found *Angels of Love* a few years ago while on Facebook, and though I was not a client, I felt instantly compelled to be part of it and partner with them. It's people like their founder, Della, who stand for what is needed in the community and advocate for the voices that go unheard.

Angels of Love fights endlessly to put a stop to domestic abuse and give survivors hope and a new life. If you or someone you know is going through this, or has a question, I urge you to pick up the phone and call them today, or please seek help. No woman should fight this alone.

I've shared with you my most vulnerable, shameful, and horrific moments of surviving domestic abuse, and being on a journey towards resilience and healing with hopes that by sharing my story, I could help at least one person and teach them to catch those red flag warnings. I come from a lineage of women who are survivors of domestic abuse, and as a mother of two beautiful daughters, I vow to protect them at all costs.

My children, grandchildren, and future generations should never find themselves victims of domestic abuse. My advice to you is, "Never stay with a man who has no respect for you, and lays a finger on you. Hold your head high and walk away, it doesn't matter how hard you fall, you will always get back up; and never lose faith and hope in yourself". Stay Strong. Stay Assertive. YOU GOT THIS GIRL!"

---My *VICTORY* Statement---

How I survived all this and lived to tell the story is a question that haunts and fuels me today! Years of suffering from a childhood of hardship, straight into adulthood still baffle me today. I have since become an advocate for women and children and have pleaded to our legislators to take action, make change, and implement laws to end abuse and protect survivors.

---Celeste---

YASMINDA'S Story...

I was raised in a traditional Catholic, Mexican household where we always had family get-togethers with music and fanfare. Though I wouldn't see them get physically aggressive, I would hear my parents argue a lot. I was a first-generation high school graduate and the first to go to college in my family. My mom would always tell me that I needed to further my education, but I didn't know how to apply or what courses to take. There were expectations but not much guidance.

In 2004, I was 23 years old and met my first ex-husband at a dance hall. Ten years later, I met my current ex-husband. We met at my workplace and started dating and got to know each other better on Facebook in 2016. I knew very little about his family, as they were very private people. What I did know was that his parents were divorced, and his sisters were very distant. Unfortunately, I also didn't know that he had clinical depression and suffered from drug addictions. I was taken back and felt very alone.

I was pregnant when we started arguing and yelling a lot. He'd often leave in the middle of the night taking my debit cards and money to go buy drugs. It was then he first got physically violent as I was telling him to stop drinking and to give up the drugs. He threw a heavy metal flashlight at me, that's how angry he got. I was standing by the baby crib in our bedroom; luckily the flashlight missed me and our son. It wasn't long before he physically struck me. I never told anyone about being hit by him as he would take my phone or would make sure to break it.

I just got home from work, one day when we got into a horrible argument. He left the house fuming so I went to look for him but couldn't find him. He ended up coming back and told me that he had slept with someone. Saddened and upset, I reached out towards him in disbelief, it was then that he punched me in the face, across my left temple. He left the house, once again.

I called his mom and told her what Carlos had done. His mother and sister came to the apartment telling me that they had heard from him and that he had plans to commit suicide. They asked me if I was going to call the police and I said, "No", that I didn't want to cause him more trouble...I didn't want to be the reason he would go through with it or be blamed.

Things would be fine for about six months, then he would hit me again. He'd be manipulative by telling me that I was a bad mother. I tried my best to keep my son safe. I finally realized that in every situation, my ex-husband always made himself to be the victim.

My parents had no idea what was going on because he started to isolate me from them. The last time a family member was at the apartment was when my sister came to help me at the birth of my son but hadn't visited again until months after that.

My ex was extremely insecure and jealous; jealousy was a big trigger for him. So much so, that I had to make sure I was out of work and on my way home by a certain time. If not, he would start to think I was cheating or I was somewhere else. He wouldn't even allow me to go to the store across the street. I started to become co-dependent.

Things got worse before everything came to light. There was a time when we were in the bedroom, and the children were playing. He picked up my 3-year-old son and hit him so hard that he left a handprint across his bottom only because he held his electronic tablet too close to his face.

I told him he didn't have to hit him that hard. Hearing that, he grabbed me and threw me on our bed. I was trying to protect myself, but he held my arms down, reared back and head-butted me right in my face. Luckily, I had my phone with me as I rushed into the kitchen to secretly take a picture and send it to an old email address then delete the evidence.

Shortly after, his father and stepmother visited but I stayed in the bedroom to hide my black eyes. After they left, I came out of my bedroom when I heard a knock on the door, and it was the local police. They said that they had received the call that I was having sexual relationships in front of my children! I asked who called to accuse me of such a terrible thing and was told that it was my ex-husband.

It sounded like something he would do. At one time, he threatened to tell the police that I was using cocaine with him so that my children would be taken away from me. Seeing the police car in the driveway, my in-laws came back and that is when they saw that he had beaten me and gave me black eyes.

He got violent again, so I finally decided to call the police. They asked me if I wanted an emergency protective order, which they initiated for 90 days to help get me back on my feet. That's when I finally decided to leave him for good. I called a Domestic Violence hotline, which directed me to a shelter agency where counseling services were offered. I soon moved my things out of our apartment and went to my parents' home.

I lived in fear throughout the day; I couldn't sleep through the night. I was afraid that he was going to find me. I realized that I needed to get my power back. Life wasn't easy after the protective order, either, I felt lost. He hadn't allowed me to work so I didn't have a job or money for a long while. I was asked what I was going to do if he tried to take the kids. I had to make sure my kids were going to stay with me. I needed help!

I followed the instructions of my counselors at the shelter agency and decided to make some personal changes. Due to stress and depression, I had become overweight, so I started to exercise and take better care of myself.

Child Protective Services (CPS) got involved and reported the incident when he hit my son and I filed a report for when he attacked and headbutted me. He was arrested because of the photo evidence that I had taken.

I followed CPS's advice and enrolled my son in school. I utilized all the resources that were provided to me as I needed all the help I could get. I started to apply for work and went to Easter Seals where they provided educational classes for me and my daughter.

I knew I wanted to give my children a happy and safe life they deserved; I needed to fight for them. Gratefully, the District Attorney's Office (DA 's office) referred me to the organization, *Angels of Love* to fight for a divorce, it was cost free!

Things are better now. My relationship with God is positive and happy. Spending more time in prayer relieved my anxiety and depression, and I have healed more with God's help. Because I don't trust my ex, I still call the local PD every time I drop off the kids for his visits.

I think about giving back to others because my kids are now growing up in a good community and I don't want to see another person, man or woman go through what I had experienced. I realized there were a lot of red flags after attending counseling sessions. One thing for sure, our relationship had moved too fast.

Advice I would give to anyone going through a relationship like this is to know and to love yourself, first. I would tell someone who is abused to have a safety plan, a support system through family, friends or church and to know that there IS always a way out. Most importantly, don't be afraid; there are people and services available to help you.

Right now, I'm in a place where I am healing with God and raising my children in a loving home. I can say that I am the happiest I've ever been since separating from my marriage five years ago. During counseling sessions, I mentioned to the counselor that I wasn't interested in getting into another relationship, if ever! But I am now open to welcoming someone into my life. If I do meet someone, I hope to grow my happy family.

During the abuse, if you were to look at the pictures of me, I truly lost myself. I was unrecognizable. Since then, I've forgiven him, but I don't associate myself with him in any way. I don't need to be anywhere I am not welcomed. I have peace for myself, and with God. I am a very proud mother; I am now strong and resilient.

I am applying for a career job at this writing. Until my hiring, I continued to spend my time volunteering at the *Angels of Love* agency, my church, and at my children's school. I thank God for every blessing that is now in my life.

---My *VICTORY* Statement---

I don't need to be anywhere I am not welcomed. I have peace for myself, and with God. I am a very proud mother; I am strong and resilient. If I meet someone, I hope to grow my happy family.

---Yasminda---

PATTY'S Story...

*J*uly 30, 2020, *was a normal* day except COVID was at high-risk. I was working from home, and my ex-fiancé was a City Commissioner in a small town in South Texas.

I had dropped off my three-year old son at daycare, which was about a 30-minute drive. I came back as he was getting ready for work. It was a very normal morning routine, as he said, "I love you" and "Have a good day.", giving me a kiss, as he left.

Midday, my ex often came home for lunch. That particular day, I had things that belonged to my dad that I needed to drop off on my way back to pick up my son, so I asked Gabe to help me load up the truck. He did and headed back to work.

Once there, I made sure to call him to let him know that I had made it there safely and that I would be heading back soon, but my message was sent straight to voicemail with a text that he would call me back. As I had planned, I headed straight home.

When I arrived, I could tell by his voice that he was angry about something and started yelling at someone on the phone. When it came to him sounding that way, I knew, whether it be about politics or anything else; the less I knew, the better.

I helped my son out of the truck and told him to go inside so his "stepdad" could finish his conversation. We headed into the bedroom to stay out of his way. I could hear my ex come in and out of the house in a quick manner. Each time the door slammed, and each heavy foot stomp on the floor sent dread through my mind and body.

Hearing him still outside, I took the chance to run to the refrigerator to check the tequila bottle he had bought just a few days ago. My heart dropped as I saw the empty bottle. I knew then it was going to be a tiring day, and a long night.

It was getting close to dinner time, and my little boy told me that he was hungry, so I cautiously went outside to let my ex know that I was going to pick up some fast food, then get ready for bed soon after. He offered his debit card, but I told him not to worry about it, that I would cover it. For some reason he got angry and started cussing at me and yelling about his ex-wife, his other kids' mom; how she "was"---always expecting him to pay for everything. I tried to tell him I understood how he felt and that I didn't mind paying for the food. I thought he would appreciate it but for some reason it made him angrier. I don't know what triggered him, but he raged!

I took that moment to grab my son and put him in the truck to head out but, as I reached the driver's side door my ex had rushed out of the house coming at us with a knife in his hand! I was confused and asked him why; his response was to puncture our tires. He kept telling me, *"Oh, you don't know who I am. You don't know what I'm capable of!!"*

I tried to talk him down by saying that I could cook something at home if he didn't want me to go anywhere. I basically said anything to try to calm him down; it was getting scary. Seeing that the neighbors stepped out of their houses at all the screaming, he quickly went into ours. I figured my ex had calmed down enough so I took my son inside and sat him on the kitchen counter to start dinner.

Hearing something behind me, I turned around and my ex-fiancé attacked me with what I realized was a *machete*! All I could think of was saving my boy as I snatched him in my arms and tried to make it to the garage door from the kitchen, all the while being slashed at. It happened so fast—the machete made contact on my poor little boy's knee, splitting it open on the downswings of striking me on the right side of my head, my face and hand! I couldn't believe what was happening!

I slipped and fell onto the floor from what I realized was a pool of blood, my and my son's blood! I lost hold of him. I'm frantic, at this time, and I can't see, maybe from the blunt cut on my frontal lobe and I see nothing but white.

I tried to get away, but my ex grabbed me, and we ended up falling to the floor, him on top of me. I struggled to get away...screaming in terror and pain... I don't recall how I got to my feet...if he got up and he yanked me up, but he then rushed like a madman into the bedroom. I realized it was my moment to escape! I ran frantically out the door to my neighbor's house, *screaming* for help...banging and kicking at their front door for them to open it. I literally fell inside their doorway as it opened, gushing blood *everywhere*.

I kept crying out, "My boy, my baby"!" thinking my son was still in the house. Thank God the police were only two-minutes down the street as the neighbors had already called them; I'm sure they weren't the only callers. Once there, an officer came straight over to help me while I shouted that my son was still inside the house! By the grace of God, just as another officer rushed towards the driveway, my son came running out of the garage towards him.

To our horror, my ex-fiancé came out running behind my little boy and started shooting at the cops. They had to quickly take cover and respond to the gunfire. My ex barricaded himself in the house for over five hours, as the officer was trying to keep me alive. I kept losing consciousness.

Waking up in the hospital after several emergency procedures I was able to see that my son was safe. But it was then that I found out that not only did my son get slashed on his knee, but that the machete had cut him above his lip, but not before gashing the top of my little boy's head, too!

With my shaven head, the deep gashes the machete caused took 24 staples to close. I was in a medically induced coma for four days and had three more procedures to also sew up slashes to the right side of my eye, neck, and fingers of the hand I tried to protect myself with. I was in the ICU for 10 long days. I wasn't told at the time, but I figured that my ex, being a hemophiliac, was dead, having bled out at the scene of the crime.

My, and my son's attack made headline news. Our trauma, emotionally and physically, outlasted the news story. In all honesty, I can't say I'm completely thriving, just yet...but I believe it was God who had gotten me through this. I am especially grateful for having my kids with me, and I need to survive for them and keep getting better.

I am still dealing with some physical repercussions, but I am grateful for surviving such an horrendous attack and prefer to rise above it. I plan to go back to school so I can work in a healing or human resource/service career. Meanwhile, I am proud to represent *Angels of Love* as Miss Angel of Love ELITE 2025!

By the time of this publication, I hope to have personally and publicly thanked the brave police officers who came to our rescue.

---*My VICTORY Statement*---

I can't say I'm completely thriving...but I believe it was God who had gotten me through this. I am especially grateful for having my kids with me, and I need to survive for them and keep getting better.

---Patty Gloria---

CATHERINE'S Story...

My story begins back in 1997. One would say it starts out much like a Cinderella tale…and in some ways it ends as such, but in a very unexpected way.

Some of my high school girlfriends and I hung out together one night and decided to go to an open concert event. Unaware of the $20 entrance charge and not having money to cover it my friends were like, hey, there's a cute guy over there at the ticket area…ask him if he'll let us in! I went up and told him that we weren't planning on staying too long. He said, "Yeah, yeah, go ahead, come on in." After we found seats in the bleachers, he came by and asked me for my number. My friends coaxed me into giving it to him; so, I did. The rest, as they say, is history.

Flash forward, we began dating, went to college and three years later decided to get married. The wedding was fit for a princess and her knight in shining armor. The fairytale wedding was attended by 500+ of all the Who's Who in Houston, Texas and the surrounding towns. My dress, breathtakingly beautiful, the décor, bar none; surely a little girl's dream wedding.

The dream continued as we had three wonderful children; our twin sons in 2004, and our daughter followed in 2008. We lived a very normal, "all-American picket-fenced" lifestyle with some perks. So, there we are, we had our beautiful 5-bedroom home, three healthy children and good careers. I worked at a bank and dreamt of owning a craft business one day; he co-owned the family construction company.

I could honestly say that I had an incredibly happy life; that is, right until my daughter's birth. I didn't know at the time, but four years into our marriage my ex-husband was often under the influence of drugs.

Year five, the verbal abuse began. That's when I noticed something was *off*. My ex's behavior towards me changed and it wasn't long until the grabbing, pushing and bruising started. For some reason, any situation would cause him to start an argument with me. This dream life was beginning to turn into a nightmare no one would ever expect.

One early morning, my world imploded. My marriage was in deep trouble. I had woken up in the middle of the night to find that my ex wasn't in bed next to me. I heard strange noises coming from the kitchen and I slowly approached and peeked in. What I saw was our beautiful six-person table *covered* with white powdery substance and weird metal pipes. I'm in my 20's, came from a humble background; we were never exposed to drugs. I married into great wealth, and I learned that day that having money comes with different challenges.

I couldn't figure out what I was seeing until it finally clicked. Though startled, he sees me and quietly says, "Go back to sleep, *you're dreaming.*" I started to cry, and in a panic said, "Okay, but *what* are you doing? He slowly, but firmly repeated, "*Go back*, go back to bed, *you're just dreaming.* Go back." I numbly headed to our bedroom, fell asleep, and woke up the next day trying to make myself believe that it truly was just a dream, but I knew it wasn't.

It was the beginning of the end of my traditional Cinderella life. I knew this situation was just too big of a problem to ignore. We were Catholic, so I started off by asking for help at the church where we got married. I told the priest we had a problem and desperately needed to talk to someone. Once they heard it was a drug-related problem I was handed a piece of paper with a name and address on it and said that it was the only person who dealt with drug matters. With the information in hand, my children and I arrived at the Woodlands location only to be told that I had to make an appointment for another day, so I did.

Long story short, I had my kids wait outside of the office door as I met with the priest. I'll never forget what he says so matter-of-factly, "Come in. Sit down. I'm going to talk to you this *one* time, and I *never* want to see you here *again*". I couldn't believe what I was hearing! Desperate, I told him that my husband was heavily involved in drugs, and I didn't know how to stop it. Could he please help? "Well, sometimes the grass isn't always greener on the other side. People think that it is, but it's not." he stated dryly, then began to scold *me*, as if it were my fault. I'm sitting there thinking, "Oh my God, this is *crazy*! I need help, and he's blaming *me*?! I quickly stood up and left with my children more desperate than when I went in.

I took it upon myself to go to another well-known church but again, no help whatsoever. Last resort, I spoke with my mother-in-law to tell her that her son had a huge drug problem, surely, she'd be concerned, right?! Instead, she was adamant and told me that I was mistaken. At that point, I truly didn't know where to go from there. I didn't want to tell my parents; they were oblivious, believing "the Cinderella-life". This went on for what seemed like forever. I felt alone and silenced.

It happened again…you might not believe it and I'll never be able to confirm, but I heard the familiar late night, early morning kitchen noise. This time, I pushed the covers away and slowly got up and out of bed; but just as my feet touched the floor I fell flat on my face. From there, I couldn't move. My body felt paralyzed. Did he drug me, I wondered. I tried to move my fingers to get the phone cord of the telephone sitting on my nightstand but couldn't. I hazily remember waking up at sunrise, my face still planted on the floor. It took a while for me to fully move my body again that day. I wish I could say it was the last time that happened, but it wasn't.

Remember my Cinderella dream turned into a nightmare? One night, things at home got frighteningly worse…I froze in fear. It happened on the night before our family trip to Seattle, WA to board an Alaskan cruise. I had cashed my paycheck and put $1,500 in my purse for shopping while on the trip. My parents came early to spend the night before catching our flight in the morning. The twins were in their bedroom next to our two guest rooms where my sister and parents stayed; I, my ex-husband and my three-year-old daughter were in our bedroom.

I noticed my ex kept waking up during the night. What is he doing? He keeps getting up from the bed. I wondered. I jumped up as it clicked, "Oh, shoot." I said, "The MONEY!" I ran to check my purse, and of course, the $1,500 was GONE! I went straight to my ex and told him that I knew he took the money. I begged him to give it back. I said, "Everybody is still asleep, no one will know, just give it to me; it's vacation money!" He started screaming at me, "What are you talking about?!" and got irate. All I could think was…Oh, my God, my parents are here, they're going to hear you! "Please, please, stop screaming!" I pleaded in a quiet panic, trying not to trigger him.

Instead, agitated and drugged up, he goes to his cabinet and grabs his gun, and points it right at me! The commotion and screaming wakes up my daughter. I'll never forget, she sits up, cries, her little legs crossed and just staring at us. Then, she stops…she doesn't speak, she doesn't say anything; she's in shock.

Hearing the pleading screams my sister wakes up. She's pounding on the door, yelling, wanting to know what's going on. "Open the door!", she yells, but I couldn't move because he had the gun to my head. All I could say as I was holding back tears, trying to be strong and not aggravate him was, "*I can't*; It's okay!". She calls out to my mom and dad, waking up the twins. Frightened by the situation they, too, demanded that I open the door… they didn't understand, I couldn't move! I thought to myself, if I move, this guy's going to kill me; and honestly, I think at that time I didn't even care anymore; but my daughter is here with me. She's watching. I worried about what the twins were thinking on the other side of the door. So, I kept begging my ex not to shoot.

Somehow with fierce adrenaline running through her, my sister broke down the door. Stunned when they saw the gun, my ex immediately pointed it at himself, and then back at me, telling them not to get close. My mom pleaded for him to give her the gun. One quick moment, my ex was distracted enough that my sister courageously ran in and grabbed my daughter, taking her safely out of the room: with my dad comforting the twins. My mom stayed with me telling my ex that we could find help for him…. like a mom would do. All the while, I can't do *anything*, I'm frozen, but shaking inside sitting on my bed, my eyes closed. He's finally going to do it, I kept thinking... But he didn't. With the plea of a mother's cry and prayers…he gave mom the gun.

When my ex was admitted into rehab, my mom asked me how long this had been going on, and if this was why I had lied about all the bruises she had asked about in the past. I was bombarded with more questions. They couldn't believe what they were hearing.

I decided to start the divorce papers after that night. While heart wrenched and frightened, I wondered if there was anyone out there who would understand what I was going through, I thought to myself, it had to be another female…surely she would understand. So, I called my sister in the Rio Grande Valley in South Texas who went through a divorce a couple of years ago, and she gave me Della's contact information. Della brought me into her office, and I told her my story; I was nervous and sobbed throughout. Della, who later founded *Angels of Love*, sat there quietly. I was taken back and so relieved that she was *listening* to me. "We can help you. I can help you.", she said. Relieved, I asked, "You will?! I told her, I didn't want my ex to get custody of my kids, and I wanted him to get help for his problem. This was a good start!

Della consoled me and told me not to be so afraid…and that everything was going to be okay. I was encouraged, but it was nerve-wracking at the same time. The day before each court date I would wake up, throw up, and have horrible stomach issues. Yes, that's how stressed out I was! I'll always remember Della telling me–looking me straight in the eyes, "…it's okay, I don't want you crying over there. Cry here…but you're going to be *strong* in the courtroom!". I was grateful for the emotional backup as it was an *ugly* divorce battle.

I'd like to take a moment to say that Della helped make me the strong woman I am today. Meeting her was the start of my personal mentorship and treasured friendship. And it was the beginning of a new and improved me.

If things weren't bad enough, I was soon diagnosed with cancer. I was beside myself with grief and gripping fear. I was angry at God, and I told Della that surely, there was *no* God; if there was, why was He punishing me like this?! Yet, I told myself that I was willing to lose it all. I didn't want to fight for *things*; I just wanted my health, my children and my freedom; and somehow, I knew God was going to help me recover from it; my sickness and my situation. My mom agreed, "…yes, don't fight him; if you and the kids are okay, just let go of everything else". I decided it was the best route to expedite the process and that was all I wanted.

I still tried to get help for my ex-husband for my children's sake and was told about a Christian church that might be able to counsel us. The pastor picked up right away that my ex didn't want to help himself. The pastor said he would keep us in prayer, and that it was time to focus on myself. I realized that I couldn't help my children's dad; it wasn't my place to. It was time to fight for my life, and I checked myself into MD Anderson Cancer Center for treatment.

Tired, but hopeful, I came back from the initial medical procedure and was told by my ex that he was not *only* going to fight for full custody of the kids, but that he was going to take the house, too! *Full custody of the children? I'm a good mom, what do you mean*, I thought?! It must have shone on my face as he blurted out, "You have cancer! You're gonna' *die*, you know! They're going to need me". He was so cruel.

Once checked in for another round of treatment, I found myself thinking all alone one night, I realized I had to rewind my whole life. I said, you know, I have to forgive him to be able to get myself better. So, I kind of talked to God that night and said, "If there's a God, if You're out there, help me; I don't want to die. Help me to get better and I'm going to change my life. I'm going to live a happy life because I'm only 28 years old!" I kept saying, "I'm too young for my life to end like this. God, help me if you're out there, help me! Make me better, please!", and He did.

Nearing the end of the divorce proceedings it was clear he was going to be awarded the house. So, I came out of MD Anderson, and I said to my ex "It's okay, take anything, just don't touch my kids." That's when I moved in with my parents; everything I owned and anything that mattered had to fit in that spare bedroom I shared with my children. "You do what you have to do."

The disastrous aftermath of the divorce was just beginning as weekend visitation was to start. My three-year-old daughter, being very attached to me, didn't want to go with her father. She would cry in a panic every time he came to pick them up. It didn't help that my ex felt the need to have not one, but *four* Sheriff vehicles surround my house and rush in to get my kids. I would beg him to stop calling the authorities, that it was very traumatic for the children, and me. He refused and continued to do things his way.

By the grace of God, with the cancer in remission, I immediately left the banking industry and started a new crafting business and a new life. Yes, I had completely lost everything but had my children and new hope. I must say, I appreciate the guidance I received earlier at the pastor's Christian church; I leaned on them a lot. They were able to get me to see things in a different way. I remember them telling me, God will take away things that aren't good enough for us. It was confirmation. So, I said to myself, okay, I'm going to forgive this guy. I went through *so* much, but I *must* forgive him and let go of all the anger to be able to make a good future for us. Another thing I realized was that, yes, he was an addict, and there *wasn't* anything that I could have done differently.

During the span of twelve challenging years, my ex did his own thing and stayed away. But, then again, he had more money selling the house; so, to him, he didn't need anyone, and my kids were an after-thought at that point. Then one day, he came back, but my kids were already grown. I wasn't scared of him anymore; but, regardless of his absence, I didn't want my children to feel abandoned by their dad or further estranged. And so, I told them, "Let's go meet your dad. You three need to visit and bond with him". The twins were close to him growing up; but my daughter didn't know much about her dad, and what she may have remembered was frightening. But I told them it was important to heal the past, establish a future and eventually forgive him. Only time could tell.

Years later, and by God's grace I remarried, which I thought I would never do again. My husband is an amazing man, a wonderful and kind person. My new life started and with this new man it continues to soar in every way with him in it.

Unexpectedly, my ex-husband reached out asking if we could be friends, just friends. "I'm married now, but you can call anytime, and my husband has no problem with it." I told him. Unfortunately, my ex explained that he was extremely ill. Here he was now, with his disability checks running out a week early every month, no vehicle, and no "status", as he was tossed aside by everyone who knew him while he was "rolling in the dough". He had lost everything and lived in a small apartment with no furniture. Having an extra bed in our spare room, I asked my husband, "Can we give him the bed and deliver it?" Every time I asked to help my ex, my husband's answer was "Okay, babe, if you want, yeah, we can do that."

One thing we would do most often is bring him hot meals. As a matter of fact, one weekend my husband asked me to call my ex and tell him that on Monday, we'd pick up wings for dinner and bring him some. My ex appreciated the offer and said, "Okay, yes, yes!" Well, that *Monday Wings Night* never came; my ex died, apparently of a massive heart attack Sunday night.

Bittersweet, that part of my life's story came to a close. We began as friends and ended up as special friends. I'm at peace knowing that Forgiveness was showered upon all of us. My boys' relationship with their dad grew to the extent of them looking out for him, buying slippers when he had none. During wintertime, they made sure he had warm clothing.

My daughter never got to tell her dad that she forgave him. She thought she had plenty of time to; but she had already made peace and forgave her dad on her own. I made sure to let my daughter know not to blame herself and that the situation wasn't her fault as she was just a baby and feared him. Everything happened the way it needed to. "Your dad and I became close, and I made sure he knew about you; Girl Scouts, your successes and graduating from college", I told her. "So, he knew about you and was so proud", I added.

I figured; that's it. That's our story of everything that happened with my ex-husband. End of story–fades into just a memory–but my prince-of-a husband came across the VCR tape of the lavish wedding with my ex and turned it into a DVD. It allowed the kids to watch my wedding to their dad. We occasionally sit together as a family and watch the happy beginning of a 12-year marriage.

I was once told, the thing about forgiveness is, it's not always just forgiving the person but releasing yourself from the bitterness of it and allowing ourselves freedom. Otherwise, unforgiveness or bitterness is like taking poison and expecting the other person to die.

A step beyond that, if we keep holding things against someone, we're not releasing *them* to move forward. So, for my ex and me, forgiveness allowed us both to change for the better, regardless of the outcome. Without forgiveness, we're hurting ourselves, double violating ourselves. And we deserve better than that.

Advice for anyone entering a relationship or going through an abusive one? There are good people out there. You don't have to accept someone who treats you badly or be stuck with that person forever if you don't leave; it might not be easy but doable. Love is out there waiting for you; start with yourself and go from there.

My Cinderella story? I was able to buy my *own* dream house and farm. I'm now living a good, quiet, and peaceful life. Ultimately, what I have learned through my story is that sometimes we have to lose it all to gain it all. God has given me back everything that I had lost–and so much more.

My three adult kids are wonderful. I look forward to one day enjoying my future grandbabies. Until then, I sell beautiful crafts and serve at our church.

---My VICTORY Statement---

Love is out there waiting for you; start with yourself
and go from there.

---Catherine---

ABOUT ANGELS OF LOVE

ANGELS OF LOVE – was founded in 2010, with the purpose of developing a full array of services for women and families who are victims of VIOLENCE. *Angels of Love* is a 501c3 nonprofit organization. *Angels of Love* fills the service gaps left by underfunded and understaffed governmental services to victims of violence. The organization's mission is "To provide victims of domestic and dating violence, sexual assault, stalking and trafficking with the tools necessary to restore each survivor to a healthy self-worth and healthy family setting". The individuals and families receiving services are experiencing or at risk of homelessness, including survivors of domestic and dating violence, sexual assault, stalking and trafficking, and other vulnerable populations.

ADVOCACY & REFERRAL SERVICES – *Angels of Love* speaks on behalf of victims to local officials, state-level officials, and federal policymakers. They work with fellow advocates and partners with other organizations that share common goals to increase our overall power and influence. *Angels of Love* provides community-based prevention activities, public awareness, legal services and legal advocacy and educational programs and initiatives.

ANGELS OF LOVE RESOURCE CENTER FOR VICTIM & FAMILY SUPPORT – *Angels of Love* also provides family support services that assist and guide parents in their role as caregivers. Such services can take many different forms depending on the strengths and needs of the family. *Angels of Love* offers the following services: **Empowerment for Victims of Domestic Violence** program which is designed to support and restore self-worth to victims of domestic violence. It focuses on fostering independence and empowering survivors to reclaim control over their lives. **Expect Respect** is a teen dating violence prevention program, **Kind Girls** is a kindness workshop for young girls, **Girl Power**

is a tween empowerment program and the **Distinguished Gentlemen Initiative,** a character-building and leadership initiative for boys.

The ***Expect Respect*TM** program works to promote healthy relationships and prevent violence and abuse among teens. The *Expect Respect* program was designed and created by The SAFE Alliance formerly SafePlace out of Austin, Texas. *Angels of Love* is the only organization south of San Antonio, Texas certified to offer the *Expect Respect* program. We provide innovative, research-based programs and training and collaborate with schools, healthcare, law enforcement, and other youth-serving organizations to create a safer environment for all young people.

Our in-school support groups, leadership programs, teen and parent presentations are effective at reducing violence and victimization. *Expect Respec*t works at the forefront of prevention and early intervention to break the cycle of abuse in teenagers' lives and prevent violence from happening in the first place. *Expect Respect* is built on an ecological and trauma-informed model that supports vulnerable youth who have already been exposed to violence, mobilizes youth leaders, and promotes safe schools and communities. *Expect Respect* engages youth, parents, schools and community organizations in promoting healthy teen relationships and preventing dating abuse.

The *Angels of Love* **Expect Respect Teen Leadership program** is designed to educate and empower teens to have healthy relationships and to become role models, allies and peer educators. Teen leaders learn to speak out about bullying, harassment and dating abuse through youth-generated projects, poster campaigns, theatre, art, music, yoga, poetry and literature. The *Expect Respect* Youth Leadership programs educate and empower youth to have healthy relationships and to become role models, allies and peer educators. Youth leaders speak out about bullying, harassment and dating abuse through youth-generated projects, campaigns, theatre, art, music and poetry. Youth Leadership Training is provided in classrooms, clubs, or other youth settings and consists of up to 8 curriculum-based sessions on preventing bullying, cyber-bullying, sexual harassment, dating abuse, and promoting healthy relationships. Lastly, the *Expect Respect* Program engages school personnel, parents and community organizations in promoting healthy relationships, creating safe school and afterschool environments and responding effectively to incidents of violence and abuse. *Expect Respect* works with schools on the development of policy, curricula, and training for administrators, counselors, faculty, nurses, coaches, law enforcement and Parent Support Specialists.

The Mission of the *Angels of Love Expect Respect* program is to educate, empower and inspire teens by raising awareness, developing communication skills and cultivating self-respect and respect for others.

The *Angels of Love* **Kind Girls** workshop for ages 6-9 is designed to inspire young girls to promote kindness and compassion towards themselves and others; thereby bringing a positive change and more happiness and pave the way to a higher self-worth. The workshop will include engaging activities and practical applications of "The Be Kind Pledge"; opportunities to put kindness into action; pay-it-forward materials, and interactive experiences to promote teamwork, self-expression, and leadership skill building.

The Mission of the *Angels of Love Kind Girls* program is to educate, empower and inspire young girls by raising awareness of being kind, developing anti-bullying and anti-bystander skills and cultivating respect for others. The program motto is **"Everywhere you go, leave a glitter trail of kindness behind you."**

The *Angels of Love Girl Power* program educates tween girls, ages 10-12, that they are valuable and have a voice that can empower them, by giving them information and tools to use. *Girl Power* helps to build confidence, competence and pride within themselves. Tween girls thrive when they receive messages of aspiration rather than limitation; when they have access to positive role models; and when they receive the resources necessary to overcome challenges. With the right people, environment, and programming, girls are empowered to set high expectations and succeed. *Girl Power* builds confidence and embraces positive decision-making, takes charge of their health and well-being, and achieves academic, personal, and career goals. As a result, they will provide themselves and their families with economic opportunity.

When girls feel confident about their bodies, beauty, uniqueness, intelligence, and worthiness they will go into the world and fully express themselves to their highest potential. *Girl Power* shows that negative self-talk keeps girls trapped in what they think the world sees, instead of embracing how they see themselves. Girl Power reinforces that they are all important, unique and can contribute to the world.

The Mission of the *Angels of Love Girl Power* program is to educate, empower and inspire tween girls by raising awareness, developing communication skills and cultivating self-respect. The motto for the program is **"Be Strong, Be Smart, Be Amazing, Be Yourself"**

The *Distinguished Gentlemen Initiative* is a character-building and leadership initiative designed for boys ages 6–12. This program emphasizes the importance of respect, kindness, and responsibility while teaching positive life skills that empower young boys to grow into compassionate and respectful young men. Through engaging workshops, mentorship, and interactive activities participants learn the values of honesty, self-discipline, empathy, and integrity—key characteristics of being a true gentleman. At its core, the program integrates domestic violence prevention by teaching boys how to foster healthy relationships, communicate respectfully, and resolve conflicts peacefully. By modeling and reinforcing these positive behaviors at an early age, the program equips boys with the tools they need to reject violence, embrace equality, and stand as allies for safe and loving homes. *The Distinguished Gentlemen Initiative* encourages participants to take pride in their character, appearance, and actions instilling confidence and a strong moral foundation. The boys learn how to tie a tie and shine their shoes, which are life skills that a true gentleman needs for the corporate world. Our boys graduate from the program not only with practical skills and leadership qualities but also with the heart and mindset to become future leaders who value respect, kindness, and non-violence in every aspect of their lives. The motto for this initiative is **"Strong Character. Kind Heart. Distinguished Gentleman."**

Angels of Love also offers **Parenting Classes**, **Financial Literacy, Conscious Choices for Change: A Batterer Intervention Prevention Program** and **EmpowerHer Initiative.** *Angels of Love* continues to expand and refine services as the need in the community grows.

Angels of Love primarily serves survivors of intimate partner violence, sexual assault, stalking and human trafficking across the Rio Grande Valley, reaching over 2,500 unduplicated adult clients with direct services annually. We service over 2,900 youth and teens through the *Angels of Love* youth programs and the Teen Dating Violence *Expect Respect* program. We reach over 9,000 people annually in the community through outreach programs and community events.

To support the programs' success, *Angels of Love* has established partnerships with local law enforcement, elected officials, school districts, non-profit organizations, legal aid providers and emergency shelters. We are actively expanding collaborations with community agencies, housing authorities and behavioral health organizations to ensure comprehensive, wraparound services for clients. Grants and community financial support are vital to the healing of our most vulnerable community members as we continue our mission to serve victims of intimate partner violence with dignity, respect, and compassion.

OUR MISSION

Angels of Love's mission is to provide victims of domestic and dating violence, sexual assault, stalking and trafficking with individualized services in a safe and loving environment to provide them with the tools necessary to restore each survivor to a healthy self-worth and healthy family setting.

OUR VISION

To be the premier organization advocating awareness and prevention of violence while leading as a transformative agent of change.

OUR VALUES

Respect

Integrity

Servant Leadership

Collaboration

Love

OUR BELIEFS

We believe it is our responsibility to empower victims of domestic and dating violence, sexual assault, stalking, and trafficking, while also inspiring our community and its leaders to act and do more.

Are you a survivor of Domestic Violence?
Your story matters. To help you begin writing *your* Victory Story, here are some thought-provoking questions to guide and inspire your reflections.

1. What was your home life growing up? Describe your parents' relationship.

2. Who were you before the abuse or trauma? Describe yourself before meeting him/her. What were you like? What were your hopes and dreams?

____

____

____

____

____

____

____

____

____

____

____

____

____

____

____

____

____

____

____

____

____

____

3. Did you experience any teen dating violence with a high school boyfriend/girlfriend? If so, describe what happened.

4. Describe how and where you met. Give as many details as you can. How old were you? How were you introduced?

5. Describe your partner's personality.

6. What kind of relationship did your partner have with their parents?

7. What do you know about your ex-partner's family life?

____

____

____

____

____

____

____

____

____

____

____

____

____

____

____

____

____

____

____

____

____

____

____

8. During your relationship, what friends did your partner have and what were they like?

----

9. Describe the first time you were exposed to domestic violence with your partner.

10. What were their triggers, if any? What was your response to their outburst?

11. Describe how you felt during this time of your life?

12. Who were you DURING the abuse? How did you change?

13. Do you have children? What did you do to keep them safe during episodes of violence? How did the violence affect them?

14. What did you do, if anything, to keep your secret from your family, co-workers and friends? Did any of them suspect that something was not right? Did anyone try to help you? Explain.

15. Describe the final straw? What was it that caused you to finally leave for good?

16. Where did you go? Who helped you escape, if anyone? Did you go back to your ex-partner after leaving? If so, how many times did you go back until you finally left for good? What was your thought process in deciding that you needed to go back after leaving the first time/other times?

____

____

____

____

____

____

____

____

____

____

____

____

____

____

____

____

____

____

____

____

____

____

____

17. After you finally escaped…What part or parts of your life did you need to rebuild? What did you do to rebuild? Did you find a better job, did you go back to school? Or learn another skill? Describe in detail.

18. Were there any community or domestic violence agencies that helped you leave your partner or in the healing and rebuilding process? Which agency helped you and what programs or services did you receive from them?

____

____

____

____

____

____

____

____

____

____

____

____

____

____

____

____

____

____

____

____

____

19. What were your triggers that caused you to remember your trauma?

20. Looking back, were there early signs in your relationship that indicated that your partner could be abusive; but that you missed? What were they?

21. What advice would you give to women entering a new relationship?

22. What advice do you have for women going through an abusive relationship?

23. Where are you on your healing journey? What did you do to heal?

24. Are you where you want to be in life? If so, what did you do to get there? If not, what do you need to work on to be living your dream life? What is next for you?

25. Who are you now? Describe yourself.

26. How is your life different? What are your hopes and dreams? Have your hopes and dreams changed?

____

____

____

____

____

____

____

____

____

____

____

____

____

____

____

____

____

____

____

____

Phoenix Warriors: *Rising From the Ashes of Domestic Violence*

All royalties from the purchase of this book go

to Angels of Love, Inc.:

Angels of Love

1305 East Nolana, Suite D

McAllen, Texas 78504

Angels of Love is a 501 (c) 3 nonprofit organization

Federal Tax Id# 74-3018501

To support our mission, donations to Angels of Love may be
made through the platforms listed below:

Angels of Love (956) 972-0685

Let's Stay Connected!

Follow *Angels of Love*
We would love to hear from you!

Angels of Love RGV

angelsoflovergv

angelsoflovergv

@Angels_of_Love